# Insects and Spiders

## Christopher O'Toole

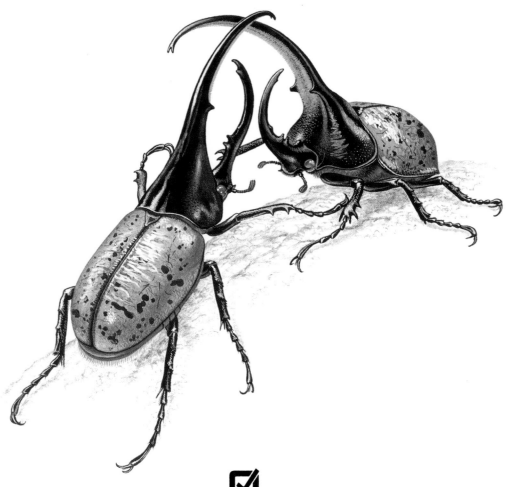

## Facts On File

*New York • Oxford*

Distributed by
**World Book, Inc.**

INSECTS AND SPIDERS
The Encyclopedia of the Animal World

Managing Editor: Lionel Bender
Art Editor: Ben White
Designer: Malcolm Smythe
Text Editor: Madeleine Samuel
Project Editor: Graham Bateman
Production: Clive Sparling, Joanna
  Turner

Media conversion and typesetting:
  Robert and Peter MacDonald,
  Una Macnamara

 AN EQUINOX BOOK

Planned and produced by:
Equinox (Oxford) Limited,
Musterlin House, Jordan Hill Road,
Oxford OX2 8DP

Prepared by Lionheart Books

Library of Congress
Cataloging-in-Publication Data
O'Toole, Christopher
  Insects and spiders/Christopher O'Toole.
  p  cm.——(Encyclopedia of the Animal
  World)
  Bibliography: p.
  Includes index
  Summary: Introduces centipedes,
    cockroaches, crickets, lice, fleas,
    butterflies, wasps, ants, scorpions, and
    other insects and spiders.

1. Insects – Juvenile literature.
2. Spiders – Juvenile literature
[1. Insects.  2. Spiders.  3. Arachnids.]
I. Title  II. Series

QL467.2.086 1989        595.7 - dc20
89-35006 CIP AC

ISBN 0-8160-1967-3

Published in North America by
Facts On File, Inc.,
460 Park Avenue South,
New York, N.Y. 10016

Origination by Alpha Reprographics Ltd,
Perivale, Middx, England

Printed in Hong Kong

10 9 8 7 6 5 4 3 2

# FACT PANEL: Key to symbols denoting general features of animals

### SYMBOLS WITH NO WORDS

**Activity time**

⬤ Nocturnal

◐ Daytime

◖ Dawn/Dusk

◯ All the time

**Adults**

Ⓦ Winged

Ⓦ Wingless

**Metamorphosis**

▢ Incomplete (young like adults)

▢ Complete (young unlike adults)

**Mouthparts**

◹ Biting

◸ Piercing and Sucking

◺ Sucking

◹ Biting and Sucking

**Conservation status**

☠ All species threatened

⚰ Some species threatened

No species threatened (no symbol)

### SYMBOLS NEXT TO HEADINGS

**Habitat**

◣ General land areas

◉ Fresh water

◉ Parasitic

**Diet**

◼ Other animals

◼ Plants

◸ Animals and Plants

**Relationship with people**

☒ Harmful

☑ Beneficial

☒ Disease vectors

☒ Crop disease vectors

⊗ Crop pests

# CONTENTS

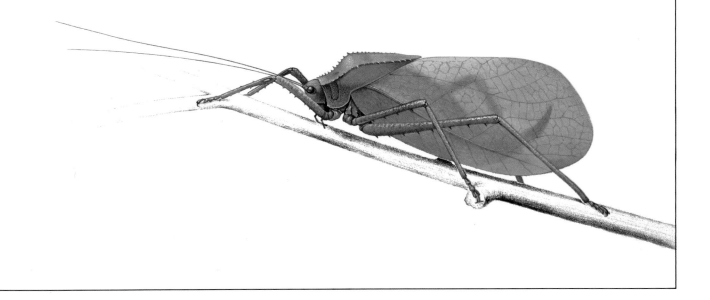

# PREFACE

### The National Wildlife Federation

For the wildlife of the world, 1936 was a very big year. That's when the National Wildlife Federation formed to help conserve the millions of species of animals and plants that call Earth their home. In trying to do such an important job, the Federation has grown to be the largest conservation group of its kind.

Today, plants and animals face more dangers than ever before. As the human population grows and takes over more and more land, the wild places of the world disappear. As people produce more and more chemicals and cars and other products to make life better for themselves, the environment often becomes worse for wildlife.

But there is some good news. Many animals are better off today than when the National Wildlife Federation began. Alligators, wild turkeys, deer, wood ducks, and others are thriving – thanks to the hard work of everyone who cares about wildlife.

The Federation's number one job has always been education. We teach kids the wonders of nature through *Your Big Backyard* and *Ranger Rick* magazines and our annual National Wildlife Week celebration. We teach grown-ups the importance of a clean environment through *National Wildlife* and *International Wildlife* magazines. And we help teachers teach about wildlife with our environmental education activity series called *Naturescope*.

The National Wildlife Federation is nearly five million people, all working as one. We all know that by helping wildlife, we are also helping ourselves. Together we have helped pass laws that have cleaned up our air and water, protected endangered species, and left grand old forests standing tall.

You can help too. Every time you plant a bush that becomes a home to a butterfly, every time you help clean a lake or river of trash, every time you walk instead of asking for a ride in a car – you are part of the wildlife team.

You are also doing your part by learning all you can about the wildlife of the world. That's why the National Wildlife Federation is happy to help bring you this Encyclopedia. We hope you enjoy it.

Jay D. Hair, President
National Wildlife Federation

# INTRODUCTION

The *Encyclopedia of the Animal World* surveys the main groups and species of animals alive today. Written by a team of specialists, it includes the most current information and the newest ideas on animal behavior and survival. The Encyclopedia looks at how the shape and form of an animal reflect its life-style – the ways in which a creature's size, color, feeding methods and defenses have all evolved in relationship to a particular diet, climate and habitat. Discussed also are the ways in which human activities often disrupt natural ecosystems and threaten the survival of many species.

In this Encyclopedia the animals are grouped on the basis of their body structure and their evolution from common ancestors. Thus, there are single volumes or groups of volumes on mammals, birds, reptiles and amphibians, fish, insects and so on. Within these major categories, the animals are grouped according to their feeding habits or general life-styles. Because there is so much information on the animals in two of these major categories, there are four volumes devoted to mammals (*The Small Plant-Eaters; The Hunters; The Large Plant-Eaters; Primates, Insect-Eaters and Baleen Whales*) and three to birds (*The Waterbirds; The Aerial Hunters; The Plant- and Seed-Eaters*).

This volume, *Insects and Spiders*, includes entries on insects, such as cockroaches, mantids, bugs, flies, fleas, beetles, moths, ants and bees, and arachnids, for example spiders and scorpions. Together they number almost 1 million species; possibly many more. It also has entries on animals closely related to insects, the millipedes and centipedes. These total another 12,000 species. The most important characteristic of all these animals is their external skeleton (exoskeleton), or cuticle. This has enabled them to live in almost every habitat, and they have become the most successful creatures on Earth. They are also all jointed-limbed creatures without backbones (invertebrates)

Insects, spiders and their allies are a vital part of the survival of all life on Earth. Some, such as ants, termites and various beetles and scorpions, dispose of dead vegetation, animal corpses and dung. Others, including bugs, crickets, grasshoppers, stick and leaf insects, comprise major plant-eaters (herbivores). In all of these roles, they process and return vast amounts of nutrients to the soil. They also form a major source of food for many meat-eating animals (carnivores), for example various birds, reptiles and mammals. As pollinators of flowers, insects such as butterflies, wasps and bees are vital links in the cycle of plant generations. However, many insects and their allies are harmful to other living things. They transmit diseases from one animal or plant to another, or eat crops and damage trees. Some of these animal diseases are deadly to people and their livestock, and the damage to vegetation can cause serious economic problems.

Whether beneficial or harmful, insects, spiders and their close relatives form essential links in the intricate web of life. Understanding their habits and ways of life is the key to the balance of nature.

Each article in this Encyclopedia is devoted to an individual species or group of closely related species. The text starts with a short scene-setting story that highlights one or more of the animal's unique features. It then continues with details of the most interesting aspects of the animal's physical features and abilities, diet and feeding behavior, and general life-style. It also covers conservation and the animal's relationships with people.

A fact panel provides easy reference to the main features of distribution (natural, not introductions to other areas by humans), habitat, diet, size, color and breeding. (An explanation of the color-coded symbols is given on page 2 of the book.) The panel also includes a list of the common and scientific (Latin) names of species mentioned in the main text and photo captions. For species illustrated in major artwork panels but not described elsewhere, the names are given in the caption accompanying the artwork. In such illustrations, animals are shown to scale unless otherwise stated; actual dimensions may be found in the text. To help the reader quickly determine the type of animal each article deals with, in the upper right part of the page at the beginning of an article is a simple line drawing of one or more representative species.

Many species of animal are threatened with extinction as a result of human activities. In this Encyclopedia the following terms are used to show the status of a species as defined by the International Union for the Conservation of Nature and Natural Resources:

Endangered – in danger of extinction unless their habitat is no longer destroyed and they are not hunted by people.

Vulnerable – likely to become endangered in the near future.

Rare – exist in small numbers but neither endangered nor vulnerable at present.

A glossary provides definitions of technical terms used in the book. A common name and scientific (Latin) name index provide easy access to text and illustrations.

# INSECTS AND THEIR ALLIES

Insects are everywhere. Not only do the number of individuals of some types (kinds or species) amount to innumerable millions, but there may even be up to as many as 30 million insect species. They are successful to say the least.

Insects are part of a huge grouping of animals known as arthropods. The name literally means "jointed feet." The arthropods include the phyla Crustacea (crabs, shrimps and lobsters), Chelicerata (spiders, scorpions, mites, horseshoe crabs) and Uniramia (centipedes, millipedes and insects).

Although this entry is primarily about insects, it includes the spiders, scorpions and their relatives, and also the centipedes and millipedes. These animals all share much of the same body plan as insects and live in very similar kinds of habitats.

If vast numbers are anything to go by, then the terrestrial (land) arthropods, especially the insects, are the most successful animals on Earth. Of the 1.2 to 1.5 million animal species that have been described, about 85 percent are insects. Furthermore, the numbers of individuals are truly staggering. For every person living today, there are estimated to be more than 200 million insects.

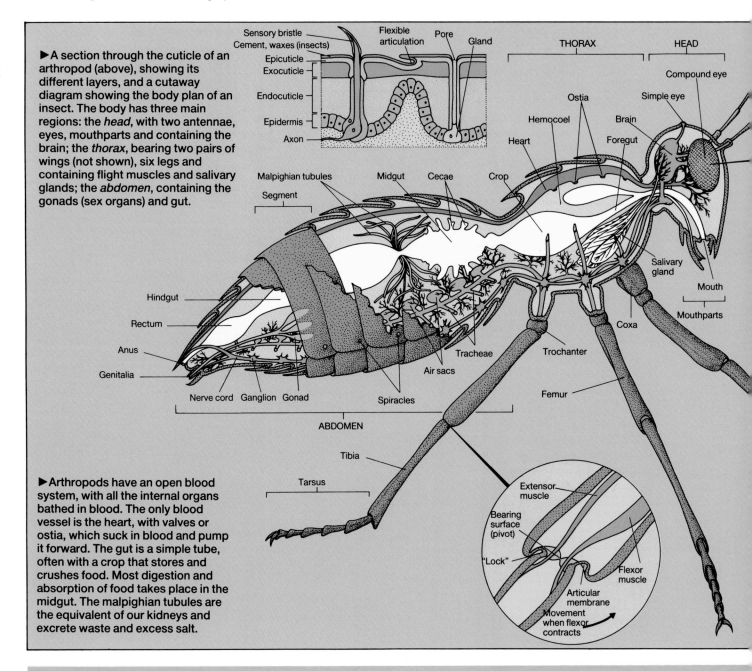

►A section through the cuticle of an arthropod (above), showing its different layers, and a cutaway diagram showing the body plan of an insect. The body has three main regions: the *head*, with two antennae, eyes, mouthparts and containing the brain; the *thorax*, bearing two pairs of wings (not shown), six legs and containing flight muscles and salivary glands; the *abdomen*, containing the gonads (sex organs) and gut.

►Arthropods have an open blood system, with all the internal organs bathed in blood. The only blood vessel is the heart, with valves or ostia, which suck in blood and pump it forward. The gut is a simple tube, often with a crop that stores and crushes food. Most digestion and absorption of food takes place in the midgut. The malpighian tubules are the equivalent of our kidneys and excrete waste and excess salt.

▲An exoskeleton of chitin provides the armor plating for this beetle, especially the elytra or wing cases.

## LIMITED ONLY BY THE COLD

Spiders are the most successful non-insect arthropods and they, too, occur in great numbers. In the countryside of temperate parts of Europe and North America, there may be as many as 2 million spiders per acre.

Together, insects and spiders have invaded all parts of the Earth except the polar regions and the tops of the highest mountains.

## A HARD EXTERIOR

Apart from having jointed limbs, all arthropods have one major feature in common: the soft parts of the body are enclosed in and protected by a hardened, external skeleton known as the exoskeleton. Much of their success can be attributed to this.

The exoskeleton is usually referred to as the cuticle and it is made of a tough, horny substance called chitin. This has a high strength-to-weight ratio and provides the sites of attachment for all the muscles the animal uses in movement.

The cuticle is arranged in a series of dorsal (upper) and ventral (lower) plates or segments, which are hinged, allowing movement between them. In many arthropods, and especially in adult insects and spiders, there is much fusion of segments for added protection. For terrestrial animals, the cuticle is important in preventing the loss of water. In small creatures, such as all insects and spiders, where the volume of the body is high relative to its surface area, water can be lost very easily and quickly.

The cuticle of spiders and insects is impregnated with a waterproof wax which reduces water loss considerably. Millipedes and centipedes do not have this wax and so must live in moist, humid places in the soil or in leaf litter.

## GROWTH PATTERN AND SIZE

Having a hard external skeleton does have its disadvantages. Growth is only possible if the cuticle is molted, or shed, periodically. Before molting, a new cuticle develops beneath the old one. When the old cuticle is shed, the new one is pale and soft and this is when growth takes place.

During this soft-bodied stage, there is a danger of water loss or attack from predators, so molting is invariably carried out in a damp and dark place.

An external skeleton also puts a severe upper limit on body size. This

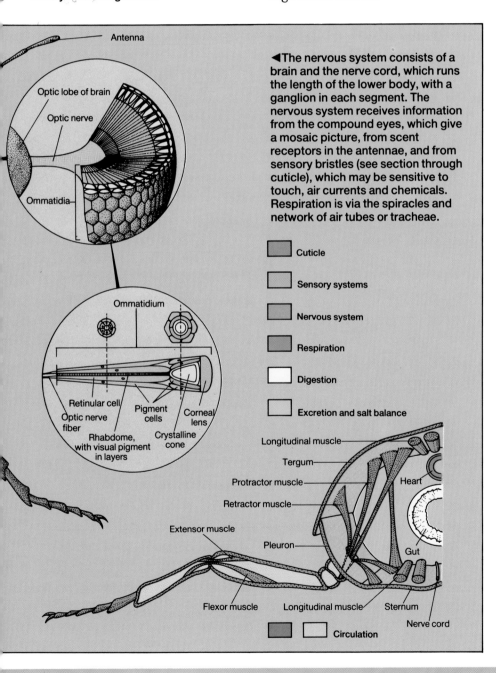

Antenna

Optic lobe of brain

Optic nerve

Ommatidia

◀The nervous system consists of a brain and the nerve cord, which runs the length of the lower body, with a ganglion in each segment. The nervous system receives information from the compound eyes, which give a mosaic picture, from scent receptors in the antennae, and from sensory bristles (see section through cuticle), which may be sensitive to touch, air currents and chemicals. Respiration is via the spiracles and network of air tubes or tracheae.

Cuticle

Sensory systems

Nervous system

Respiration

Digestion

Excretion and salt balance

Ommatidium

Retinular cell

Optic nerve fiber

Pigment cells

Corneal lens

Rhabdome, with visual pigment in layers

Crystalline cone

Longitudinal muscle

Tergum

Protractor muscle

Heart

Retractor muscle

Extensor muscle

Pleuron

Gut

Flexor muscle

Longitudinal muscle

Sternum

Nerve cord

Circulation

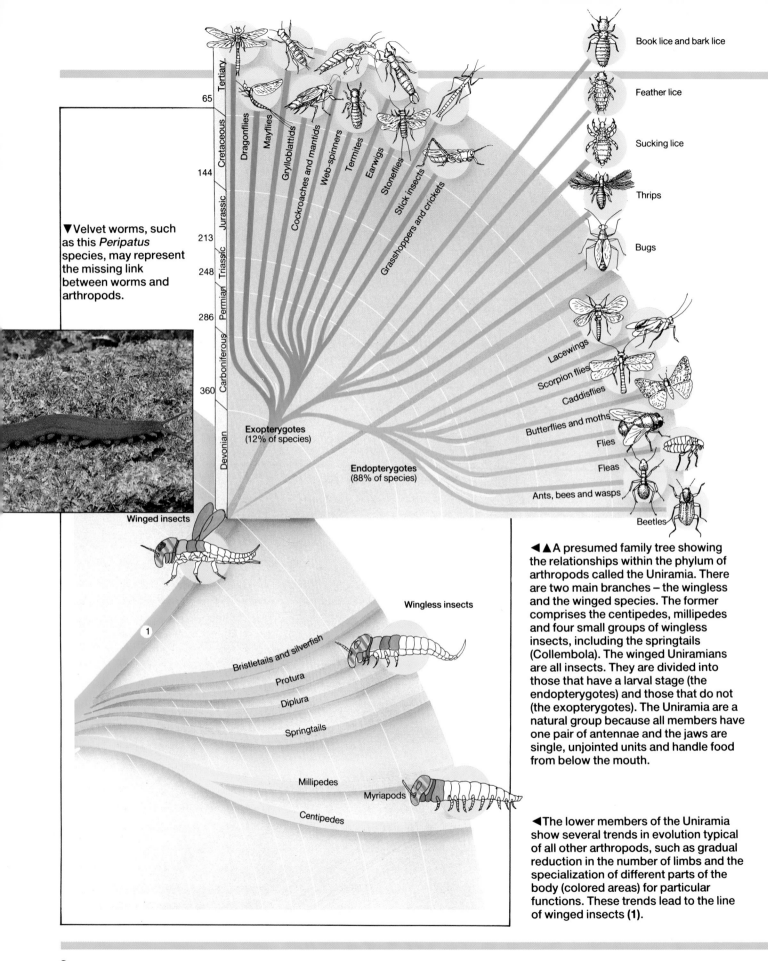

65

Tertiary

Cretaceous

144

Jurassic

213

Triassic

248

Permian

286

Carboniferous

360

Devonian

Dragonflies

Mayflies

Grylloblattids

Cockroaches and mantids

Web-spinners

Termites

Earwigs

Stoneflies

Stick insects

Grasshoppers and crickets

Book lice and bark lice

Feather lice

Sucking lice

Thrips

Bugs

Lacewings

Scorpion flies

Caddisflies

Butterflies and moths

Flies

Fleas

Ants, bees and wasps

Beetles

Exopterygotes
(12% of species)

Endopterygotes
(88% of species)

Winged insects

▼Velvet worms, such
as this *Peripatus*
species, may represent
the missing link
between worms and
arthropods.

Wingless insects

①

Bristletails and silverfish

Protura

Diplura

Springtails

Millipedes

Myriapods

Centipedes

◄▲A presumed family tree showing
the relationships within the phylum of
arthropods called the Uniramia. There
are two main branches – the wingless
and the winged species. The former
comprises the centipedes, millipedes
and four small groups of wingless
insects, including the springtails
(Collembola). The winged Uniramians
are all insects. They are divided into
those that have a larval stage (the
endopterygotes) and those that do not
(the exopterygotes). The Uniramia are a
natural group because all members have
one pair of antennae and the jaws are
single, unjointed units and handle food
from below the mouth.

◄The lower members of the Uniramia
show several trends in evolution typical
of all other arthropods, such as gradual
reduction in the number of limbs and the
specialization of different parts of the
body (colored areas) for particular
functions. These trends lead to the line
of winged insects **(1)**.

is for two reasons. First, a large animal would collapse under its own weight immediately after molting, before the new cuticle had time to harden.

Second, the way terrestrial arthropods breathe is efficient only within certain size limits. Insects, millipedes and centipedes all breathe through openings along the sides of the body called spiracles. From each spiracle a system of fine tubes lined with cuticle radiates to all parts of the body. These tubes, known as tracheae, allow oxygen to spread inwards and the waste gas, carbon dioxide, and water vapor to spread outwards.

## HEART-LUNG SYSTEM

Most spiders, too, possess a system of tracheae. The breathing tubes radiate from a spiracle at the rear of the abdomen. But they also have another respiratory structure called a book lung. This is a chamber in the underside of the abdomen that opens via a single hole. Inside, there are stacks of folds, or leaves, rather like the pages of a book, hence the name. The leaves alternate with air spaces. The heart pumps blood through the stacks and oxygen is absorbed across the thin leaf membrane. At the same time, carbon dioxide passes from all the leaves, into the spaces and out of the body.

Above a certain body size, the ratio of volume to surface area becomes too great. To use either a system of tracheae or a book lung in order to breathe, the whole body cavity would have to be given over to these structures and there would be no room for any other organs. Hence, very few arthropods grow to more than 4in long and the majority are less than 1in in length.

Apart from the exoskeleton and tracheae, chitin also lines the front and rear ends of the gut, and parts of the genital system. It is a truly remarkable and adaptable substance and can be exist in many forms, from the heavy armor plating of large beetles, to the delicate, coiled proboscis of moths and butterflies.

## TWO WAYS OF GROWING UP

About 12 percent of insects have a kind of development called incomplete metamorphosis. In this, the egg hatches to produce a larva or nymph, which is a miniature version of the adult. The larva molts several times before becoming adult. Small wing buds appear in the later larval stages. Because the wings develop externally, these insects all form a sub-group of insects known as the Exopterygota. Often, the larva and adult live in the same place and eat much the same kind of food.

The exopterygotes include insects such as the dragonflies (Order Odonata), cockroaches (Blattodea), crickets and grasshoppers (Orthoptera) and the true bugs (Hemiptera).

The other 88 percent of insects all have a much more advanced type of development called complete metamorphosis. Here, after the larva has molted its skin perhaps five times, there is a non-feeding stage, the pupa, before the insect becomes adult.

**INSECT FACTS**
**Smallest:** Parasitic wasp (Fairy fly) *Prestwichia aquatica*, length ¹⁄₁₀₀in.
**Bulkiest:** Goliath beetle (*Goliathus druryi*), length up to 8in, weighs more than a small bird such as a sparrow.
**Longest:** Giant Australian stick insect (*Extatosoma tiaratum*), 13in.
**Fastest flying:** Giant hunting wasp (*Editha magnifica*), 48mph.
**Fastest wingbeat:** Midge species, *Forcipomyia*, 1,046 beats per second.
**Largest wingspan:** Oriental Atlas moth (*Attacus atlas*), 12in.
**Fastest runner:** Tiger beetle (*Cicindela* species), 24in per second.
**Most poisonous:** South African velvet ant (mutillid wasp) (*Traumatomutilla* species).

◀This male African moon moth, *Argema mimosae*, displays its highly sensitive green antennae. These smell sensors can detect chemicals produced by virgin females over distances of 450yd or more.

Inside the pupa, most of the tissues are broken down gradually to feed special areas of cells that develop into adult structures. Insects with this kind of development are called End-opterygotes, because the wings form inside the body. All the higher insects are endopterygotes and typical examples are the flies (Diptera), beetles (Coleoptera), butterflies and moths (Lepidoptera), and the wasps, bees and ants (Hymenoptera).

## SOME REASONS FOR SUCCESS

Because they all share approximately the same body plan (see pages 6-7), arthropods were, until quite recently, thought to make up a single, natural grouping of animals which had a common worm-like ancestor. But it is now widely accepted that the three major phyla all arrived at the arthropod body plan independently, from quite different worm-like ancestors.

There is no doubt that of the many arthropods, insects have made the most of the advantages conferred by this body plan. In searching for the reasons why insects are so successful, we can best start by looking at the one habitat where they have been dismal failures, the sea. Although a few species of insect live on the sea surface, even fewer spend their lives in the water.

It is unlikely that living in salt water is the difficulty. After all, some insects live in equally harsh environments, such as in crude oil. If one looks at the things insects do, one may find an answer. Insects run about on their many-jointed legs, and most can fly. Many scavenge on dead plants and animals. Others eat living plants or

◀Development in the Orchard butterfly, *Papilio aegus*, of Australia: a newly hatched larva eats its egg shell; second stage larva with its molted skin; older larva displaying foul-smelling red filaments to deter predators; pupa, hanging from leaf stem by a silk thread.

hunt other insects and other small animals. Some species graze on algae, lichen and mosses.

## CONQUERING SEA AND LAND

In the sea, all of these activities are performed by another group of animals with jointed legs, the Crustacea. We can even regard swimming to be the crustacean's version of flying.

Fossils suggest that the first of the crustaceans appeared in the Cambrian period, 600 to 500 million years ago. The first insect fossils are younger and date from the Devonian period, 400 to 360 million years ago. Thus, the ancestors of modern shrimps, crabs and lobsters were performing all these tasks long before insects appeared.

Insects, of course, have conquered the land. Crustaceans, mostly, have not. While it is true that there are land crabs and that the familiar woodlice are crustaceans, both survive for the most part only in dark, damp places.

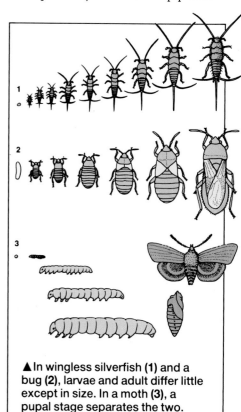

▲In wingless silverfish (1) and a bug (2), larvae and adult differ little except in size. In a moth (3), a pupal stage separates the two.

◀The dense fur of this moth, *Acraga moorei*, keeps in the heat generated by the flight muscles, so its body temperature is higher than the outside air. This enables the insect to keep flying when the temperature drops.

▼Rain is very rare in deserts, so this desert beetle, *Onymacris unguicularis*, collects water droplets condensing on its body from early morning mist.

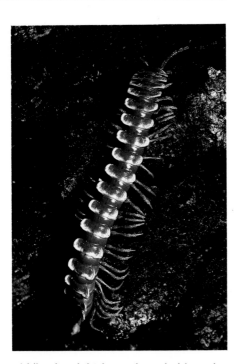

▲Like the eight-legged arachnids and six-legged insects, this many-legged millipede, walks by wave-like movements of its jointed limbs.

## LIVING IN HARMONY

When we state that crustaceans and insects are successful, we are really indicating that these animals have invaded and occupied a huge range of niches – the crustaceans in the sea, the insects on land.

A niche is all the things an animal needs to survive and reproduce: time, space, warmth, food, mates. It also includes the unique way each species uses these things. In other words, a niche is also an animal's life-style. No two species are identical in the way they use these vital resources; no two species do the same things. Because of this, many closely related and similar species can share the same habitat, each occupying its own niche.

## HOW DO THEY DO IT?

Why have insects been able to occupy so many of the important niches in the world? One obvious answer is their size. Many niches are unavailable to large animals such as cats and cows.

Neither can exploit any of the livings to be made in the soil, under stones, under bark, inside wood, in the tree canopy. But insects, being smaller, can get in these places and live and breed.

Another reason for the success of insects is their ability to fly well. This enables them quickly to find new food sources, escape predators, and to disperse. Many dragonflies, moths and butterflies regularly migrate for long distances to avoid extremes of temperature and also to find suitable places to bring up their young. Dispersal also opens up the possibility of colonizing new habitats and occupying new niches allowing them to evolve into new species.

In the isolated islands of Hawaii, there are 6,500 native insect species. It has been estimated that these are the descendants of just 250 species that were able to cross the Pacific Ocean by chance in the 800,000 years since these volcanic islands first arose from the Pacific seabed.

## INSECTS AND THE ECOSYSTEM

Insects are an important part of the life support system of our planet. They perform many vital roles. They dispose of dead and rotting plants and animals and, in so doing they return nutrients to the soil. Insects are the only food of a wide range of larger animals. As predators, they kill many pest insects. Lastly, as pollinators of flowering plants, they are important in crop production and maintaining much of our vegetation.

Although some species are pests to crops and others spread human and animal diseases, the scale is tipped very much in the insects' favor.

Finally, it is helpful to remember that our earliest human ancestors inherited a range of habitats largely shaped by all the inter-relationships between insects, plants and other animals. Life on this planet can get along well without people, but it cannot, in its present forms, do without insects. Without them, we would die.

# MILLIPEDES, CENTIPEDES

It is a mild, humid night in a wood. Soon after dark, convoys of many-legged creatures emerge from the leaf litter and make their way up tree trunks. Some are slow-moving and cylindrical, and they constantly tap the bark with their short antennae. They are millipedes, grazing on algae. Others are more nimble, with fewer but longer legs. They are centipedes, on the prowl for insects and other small prey.

---

## MILLIPEDES, CENTIPEDES Superclass Myriapoda (*11,000 species*)

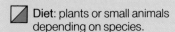 **Habitat:** leaf litter, soil, under stone and bark.

**Diet:** plants or small animals depending on species.

**Relationship with people:** some beneficial – centipedes kill many pests; some millipedes damage crops, a few centipedes give a painful bite.

**Distribution:** almost worldwide.

**Size:** length 1/25-13in.

**Color:** mainly brown or black.

**Species mentioned in text:**
Australian red-footed centipede (*Ethmostigmus rubripes*)
Blue-keeled millipede (*Polydesmus* species)
Common black millipede (*Tachypodiulus niger*)
Giant millipede (*Epibolus pulchripes*)
Pale-footed flat-backed millipede (*Strongylosoma pallipes*)
Rock millipedes (e.g., *Callipus longobardius*)
Stone centipedes (*Lithobius* species)

---

Millipedes and centipedes are mostly secretive creatures that hide away in dark, damp places during the day. Unlike the insects, their cuticle (skin) has no wax and they are liable to death by drying out. It is at night that they come into their own and act out their lives as plant- or meat-eaters.

Popular belief has it that centipedes have a hundred legs and millipedes have a thousand legs: in parts of North America, millipedes are actually called "thousand-leggers." In fact, according to species, centipedes have between 15 and 70 pairs of legs, while millipedes may have 20 to 200 pairs.

### WORM- AND INSECT-LIKE
Together with the insects and several smaller, lesser known groups, all the millipedes and centipedes make up the phylum Uniramia. This is believed to be a natural grouping of animals that possess a common, worm-like ancestor shared by no other group.

Uniramians have in common one pair of antennae, unbranched limbs, and jaws that are single, unjointed limbs. These pick up food from below the mouth. Within the Uniramia, the millipedes (class Diplopoda) and centipedes (class Chilopoda) form the superclass Myriapoda (which means many-footed) and are often referred to as myriapods.

Millipedes and centipedes all have simple eyes, or ocelli, the numbers of which vary according to the species. Some centipedes have dense concentrations of ocelli that look like the compound eyes of insects, but there is no evidence that they form an image. It seems that like other ocelli, they simply detect light and dark. The antennae detect both scent and touch. Many centipedes have long hind legs, which function as extra antennae.

▶A mating pair of Giant millipedes in Kenya. The brilliant warning colors signal to would-be predators that the millipedes are protected by poisons.

### THE PLANT-EATERS
Millipedes can be distinguished from the centipedes at a glance. Although both kinds of animal have long, thin bodies divided into segments, only the millipedes have two pairs of legs per segment. Millipedes have simple chewing mouthparts and do not have the massive poison fangs sported by the carnivorous centipedes.

The shape of a millipede's body is adapted to precisely where it lives. Thus, species which spend most of their time in cracks in the soil, such as the Blue-keeled millipede, are rather flattened. Others are very smooth and

▲ This warningly-colored South African millipede is coiled up for protection. Birds such as quails sometimes eat millipedes with no bad effects.

cylindrical in shape, with a rounded head, and are well adapted for bull-dozing their way through soil.

Most millipedes are plant-eaters, feeding on partly decomposing plants or grazing on algae encrusting tree trunks. A few species eat the roots of living plants and can be pests in gardens. In woodlands, millipedes are very important because they recycle nutrients, returning them to the soil via their droppings and, eventually, as their dead bodies.

Tropical plant-sucking millipedes have mouthparts modified to form a long beak, which they use to pierce plant stems and suck up the juices. In their diet and digestion, a few species resemble earthworms and eat soil, extracting nutrients as the soil passes through the gut.

## ODD ONES OUT

The rock millipedes have all become predators. They prey on earthworms, harvestmen, centipedes and insects. They are also unusual for millipedes in yet another way: because of their feeding habits, they have to be able to move quickly. One species can cover 3in in a second, which is twice as fast as other millipedes.

While most millipedes do not have a waxy layer to their cuticle, a few species that live in deserts do have such protection against drying out. Despite this, they have to modify their behavior to avoid the worst of the dry heat. They spend the days in rock crevices and under stones and only come out at night. Some rock millipedes are slightly better adapted for desert life. They have special sacs at the bases of their legs, which they use to take up drops of dew in the early parts of the mornings.

The Common black millipede of Europe avoids extremes of climate by burrowing into soil or rock crevices or under bark in hot dry weather.

It will also readily crawl out of these places if they become waterlogged after heavy rain.

Unlike insects, millipedes are unable to close the spiracles through which they breathe, and there is the danger of drowning. Millipedes therefore live on a knife's edge and always have to move to where there are survivable conditions.

## SPEEDY AND POISONOUS

Centipedes have longer legs than millipedes and most species are built for running. Only the blind, thread-like burrowing kinds resemble the millipedes in their slow, crawling gait and numerous short legs.

All centipedes are predators. They prey on worms, snails and insects. The largest tropical species grow to as long as 13in and prey on lizards, frogs, toads and small mice.

Centipedes are superbly equipped for life as predators. Apart from a rapid turn of speed, they are armed with a powerful pair of curved poison fangs containing venom glands. These are really the modified legs of the first segment of the body.

▼ Built for speed, this large centipede from Australia is a fearsome nocturnal hunter in the deserts. One of the poison fangs can be seen at the side of the head.

A centipede detects prey with its antennae and legs. It seizes the victim with its poison fangs and then injects the animal with venom. The poison fangs continue to grip the prey while the jaws and other mouthparts manipulate it for feeding.

## MATING FROM A DISTANCE

Male millipedes court their mates in a variety of ways. Some emit sexual scents or pheromones and indulge in much tapping and drumming of the female's head with their antennae. In the cylinder centipedes, the male signals to the female by climbing on her back, using special pads on his legs. The males of other species make rasping sounds by rubbing parts of the body together.

The males of both millipedes and centipedes transfer sperm indirectly. This means that the male's genital organs do not contact or enter the female. A male millipede first passes its sperm to specially modified legs called gonopods. Usually, these are on the seventh body segment. During mating, the male inserts the gonopods into the female's genital opening and sperm are transferred in this way.

Male centipedes do things differently. They do not mate at all. Instead, after a male has found a receptive female, he makes a little web of silk from glands near his genital opening. He then lays a sperm package called a spermatophore onto the web. The female then picks this up and puts it in her genital opening.

## PLAYING IT SAFE

Before the male centipede spins his web and deposits his spermatophore, he may court the female for up to an hour. With such voracious predators, it pays both sexes to be careful about recognition. Courtship often involves both sexes circling each other. In the stone centipedes, the male places his hind pair of legs either side of the spermatophore web, turns around

and strokes the female's antennae with his own to gain her favor.

## PARENTAL CARE

Female millipedes lay from 10 to 300 eggs, often in a little cup made of their own droppings. Some species, such as the Pale-footed flat-backed millipede, make nest chambers in the soil and reinforce the walls with repeated applications of their own excreta. The females make several of these nests and lay 40 to 50 eggs in each.

Many female centipedes lay eggs singly in the soil, but some, such as the burrowing centipedes, guard their clusters of 15 to 35 eggs until they hatch and the young disperse.

## NO TRUE LARVAL STAGE

Millipedes and most centipedes hatch from the egg with only part of the full number of adult body segments. These increase with each molt until the full complement is finally reached at adulthood. Only those centipedes that guard their young have the full number of segments on hatching.

Centipedes may take several years to reach sexual maturity. Millipedes are also long-lived, with lifespans of 10 or more years in some species.

▼The "leg waves" down the side of this tropical millipede's body are clearly visible as it browses on rotting leaves on the forest floor.

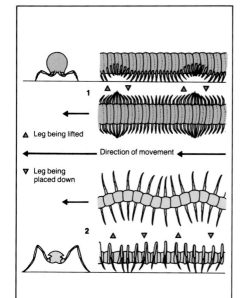

▲ Leg being lifted

Direction of movement ◄

▼ Leg being placed down

▲How to avoid tripping over many feet. Both millipedes and centipedes move by wave-like movements of the legs along the body. In the slow-moving cylinder millipede (1), the leg waves on both sides of the body are in phase. The stroke of each leg is long and most of the legs are in contact with the ground. A single wave of leg movements may involve 22 or more pairs of legs, and the relatively rigid body remains straight when in forward motion. In fast-running centipedes (2), the leg waves on both sides of the flexible body are out of phase and the body bends from side-to-side. Each leg stroke is short and fewer legs are in contact with the ground.

# DRAGONFLIES, DAMSELFLIES

Dragonflies hawk and dart up and down a slow-moving, weed-filled river. Their aerial acrobatics catch the eye, for these wingborne hunters are brightly colored. Fluttering among the waterside weeds are their more delicate relatives, blue and red damselflies. They, too, hunt various insect prey on the wing.

The body plan of dragonflies and damselflies has remained virtually unchanged since the Carboniferous period, 345-280 million years ago. But no modern species can match some giants of the Carboniferous, which had wingspans of up to 30in. Today, the largest species is one of the giant damselflies of South America, with a wingspan of about 7in.

Dragonflies and damselflies have long, thin bodies and large mobile heads with enormous eyes and very powerful jaws. There are two pairs of wings each with a complex network of veins.

Dragonflies are usually larger, faster and more powerful fliers than damselflies. When at rest, they hold their wings outspread, while damselflies fold their wings over their bodies.

## HUNTING ON THE WING

Dragonflies and damselflies prey on other flying insects, especially small flies, but also bees and flying beetles. Everything about them is geared to hunting on the wing. They have good vision, with some species being able to detect the slightest movement from a distance of 60ft. They can accelerate quickly in the air, and some have been recorded flying at 14mph. As well as rapid turns of speed, they can hover, fly backwards or even loop-the-loop.

The insects' hunched-up thorax contains the powerful flight muscles; the six spiny legs hang forward in a grasping fashion and act as a kind of aerial trawl for catching insects. Large dragonflies, like the Brown hawker, may grab small frogs from the ground, and damselflies often pluck up aphids and beetle larvae from plants.

## WHEELS AND TANDEMS

In many species of dragonfly each male adopts and patrols a territory around a pond or along a riverbank. The territory usually contains suitable egg-laying sites for the females. A territorial male defends his patch

►A female Broad-bodied darter dragonfly rests on a waterside plant. Her wing veins are very prominent.

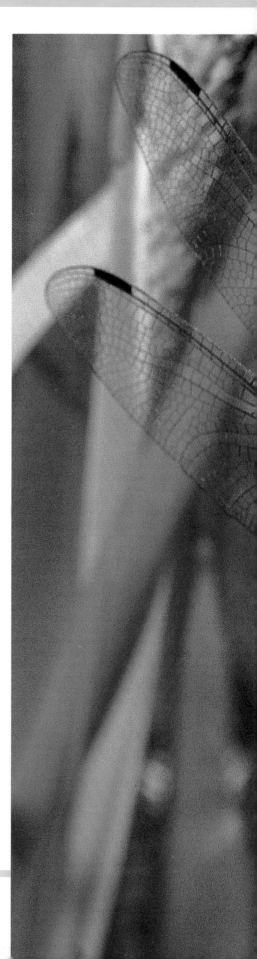

---

## DRAGONFLIES, DAMSELFLIES
Order Odonata (*about 5,000 species*)

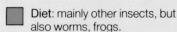 **Habitat:** larvae aquatic; adults aerial, usually near water, but often migrate some distance away.

**Diet:** mainly other insects, but also worms, frogs.

**Relationship with people:** beneficial – eat some plant pests.

Distribution: worldwide.

Size: length ¾-6in, wingspan 1-7in.

Color: drab browns to bright blue, green, yellow, red, often metallic.

Species mentioned in text:
Banded demoiselle (*Calopteryx splendens*)
Broad-bodied darter dragonfly (*Libellula depressa*)
Brown hawker dragonfly (*Aeshna grandis*)
Giant damselflies (*Megalopropus* species)

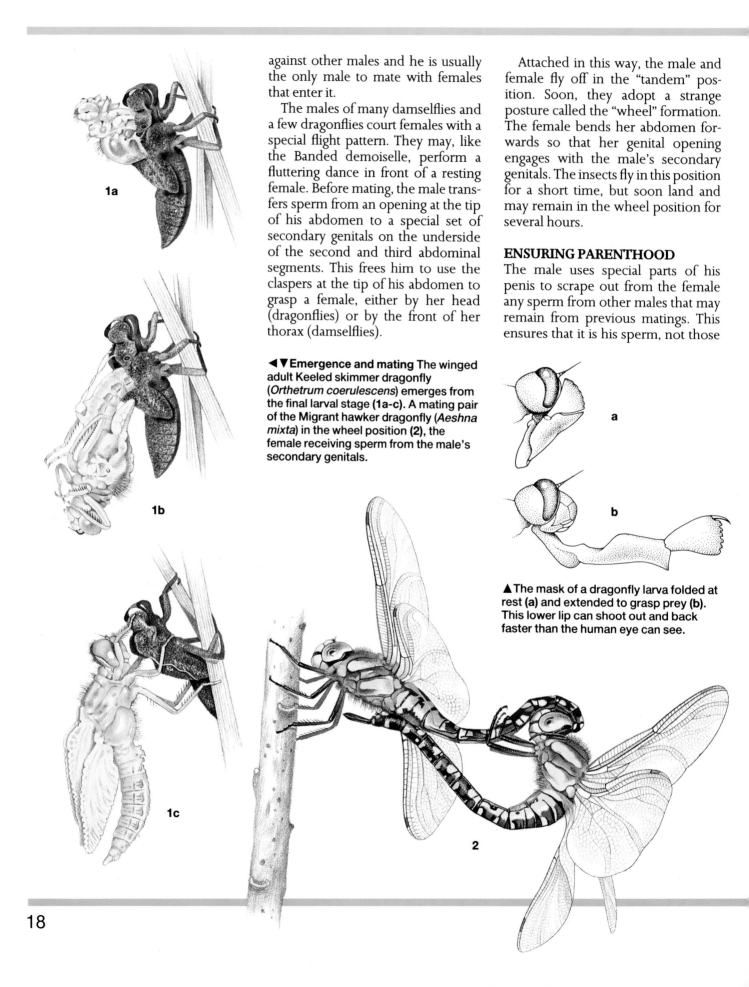

against other males and he is usually the only male to mate with females that enter it.

The males of many damselflies and a few dragonflies court females with a special flight pattern. They may, like the Banded demoiselle, perform a fluttering dance in front of a resting female. Before mating, the male transfers sperm from an opening at the tip of his abdomen to a special set of secondary genitals on the underside of the second and third abdominal segments. This frees him to use the claspers at the tip of his abdomen to grasp a female, either by her head (dragonflies) or by the front of her thorax (damselflies).

Attached in this way, the male and female fly off in the "tandem" position. Soon, they adopt a strange posture called the "wheel" formation. The female bends her abdomen forwards so that her genital opening engages with the male's secondary genitals. The insects fly in this position for a short time, but soon land and may remain in the wheel position for several hours.

### ENSURING PARENTHOOD

The male uses special parts of his penis to scrape out from the female any sperm from other males that may remain from previous matings. This ensures that it is his sperm, not those

◄▼**Emergence and mating** The winged adult Keeled skimmer dragonfly (*Orthetrum coerulescens*) emerges from the final larval stage (**1a-c**). A mating pair of the Migrant hawker dragonfly (*Aeshna mixta*) in the wheel position (**2**), the female receiving sperm from the male's secondary genitals.

▲The mask of a dragonfly larva folded at rest (**a**) and extended to grasp prey (**b**). This lower lip can shoot out and back faster than the human eye can see.

of a rival, which fertilize the eggs of his mate. The males of several species remain in tandem with their mates while they lay eggs.

## UNDERWATER DRAGONS

The larvae of dragonflies and damselflies live and grow in and around water. Many are found in still ponds, others in fast-flowing streams, while a few live among the damp leaf litter of forests.

The larvae are drab, brownish-gray, mottled creatures. Their ugliness gives no hint of the adult beauty to come. They creep about on the muddy bottoms of ponds and rivers, or among water weeds.

Damselfly larvae are slender, and each has three leaf-shaped gills at the tip of the abdomen. These absorb oxygen from the water and allow waste carbon dioxide to pass out of the insects. The larvae swim with a side-to-side motion and the gills help by acting like paddles.

Dragonfly larvae have internal gills hidden in a chamber at the end of the gut. They breathe by sucking water into the chamber and then squirting it out. This enables the larvae to dart forward in a kind of jet propulsion and is a means of escape from such enemies as fish.

Larval dragonflies and damselflies prey on many small water creatures, including worms, snails, water fleas, other insect larvae, tadpoles and small fish. They catch prey using their lower lip, or labium, which is highly modified and hinged, forming a structure called the mask. Two hooks at the end of the mask spear the victim and bring it within reach of the jaws.

When fully grown, the larvae climb up the stem of a water plant into the air and shed their skin for the final time to reveal the adult dragonfly or damselfly. The final body colors may take several days to develop. Meanwhile, the young adult feeds and improves its flying skills.

▲**Egg-laying and hatching** Without the help of her mate, a female Golden-ringed dragonfly (*Cordulegaster boltonii*) **(1)** uses her ovipositor specially modified for laying eggs in gravelly streams. A male Azure damselfly (*Coenagrion puella*) **(2)** helping a female to lay her eggs. On her own, this female Southern hawker dragonfly (*Aeshna cyanea*) **(3)** lays an egg in a water-logged stump. An adult Azure damselfly **(4)** hatches.

# COCKROACHES

It is 7pm in a Chicago hospital. The night staff have arrived for duty. Although the kitchen is now in darkness, another, six-legged, night shift begins its work. Cockroaches scavenge in warm nooks and crannies for tiny leftover crumbs of food. Meanwhile, in New York City, a television set loses its picture in a shower of sparks; cockroaches have chewed through the insulation of some vital wires.

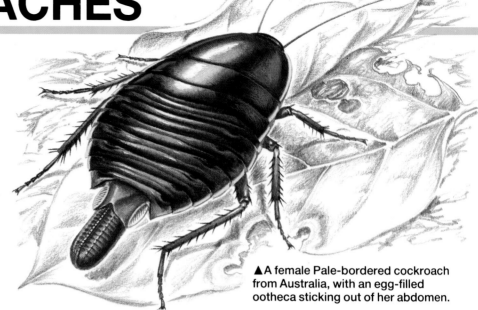

▲A female Pale-bordered cockroach from Australia, with an egg-filled ootheca sticking out of her abdomen.

## COCKROACHES Order
Blattodea *(about 3,500 species)*.

   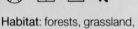

 **Habitat:** forests, grassland, desert, mountains, tundra.

**Diet:** generally omnivorous, scavenging; some eat wood.

**Relationship with people:** nuisance pests, some spread disease.

**Distribution:** worldwide, except polar regions.

**Size:** length ½-2⅓in.

**Color:** mainly dark; drab browns and grays, a few brightly colored.

Species mentioned in text:
American cockroach (*Periplaneta americana*)
Beetle-mimicking cockroach (*Paratropes lycoides*)
Brown-hooded cockroach (*Cryptocercus punctulatus*)
German cockroach (*Blatella germanica*)
Gray cockroach (*Nauphoeata cinerea*)
Oriental cockroach (*Blattella orientalis*)
Pale-bordered cockroach (*Polyzosteria limbata*)
Viviparous cockroach (*Diploptera punctata*)

Cockroaches eat almost anything and are found nearly everywhere. They have colonized many kinds of habitat from forests, swamps and grasslands to deserts. They range from sea level to the tops of mountains up to 6,500ft high. Fossils from the Carboniferous period, 345-280 million years ago, show that cockroaches have been around for a long time.

### SUITED TO THEIR HABITAT
All cockroaches have tough chewing mouthparts. Many species, including those found in buildings, tend to have smooth flat bodies. They are ideally suited for living in narrow crevices behind ovens and cupboards. The head is protected and largely hidden by a shield-like plate. The spiny legs are long and adapted for running.

Those cockroaches that live in trees are slender and have well-developed wings and long thin legs. Burrowing species are stocky, wingless, and with short, stubby spade-like legs covered with thick spines.

Most cockroaches are nocturnal and live on the ground among leaf litter, where they eat living and dead plant and animal material. The Brown-hooded cockroach of North America

▼By clustering together, each of these cockroach nymphs reduces its chances of being eaten by a predator.

is a true specialist; it feeds on wood. But this is tough, and contains cellulose, which is virtually indigestible. However, the cockroach gets around this problem by being host to some special single-celled animals (protozoa). These live in the gut and digest the cellulose for it.

## INSECT RATS AND MICE

Several species live in close association with people. These include the very familiar American, Oriental and German cockroaches.

Despite its name, the German cockroach most probably came from the tropics. With its flattened body, it can crawl unnoticed into tiny crevices and so, like the American and Oriental cockroaches, was easily transported accidentally all over the world by migrating people, in baggage or in cargo on ships.

These insect vermin prefer warm places such as bakeries, kitchens and hospitals. They can be a serious hazard to health; like rats and mice, they eat rotting matter, and can spread diseases if they enter kitchens and walk over exposed food.

## ATTRACTING A MATE

In many species of cockroach, males attract females by emitting a special scent called a pheromone. In the Gray cockroach of North America, for example, the female eats a special fluid produced by the male just before she mates with him. This probably provides a nutrient she needs in order to make eggs.

The female of the German cockroach, like many species, lays up to 40 eggs at a time in a little package called an ootheca, which she secretes from glands in her abdomen. She carries

▲ With identical warning colors to those of a poisonous lycid beetle, this South American Beetle-mimicking cockroach avoids being eaten by birds.

the ootheca sticking out of the end of her abdomen until the eggs are ready to hatch to produce larvae.

## GROWING UP

In most cockroach species, the larvae look like miniature versions of their parents and are known as nymphs. They eat the same kinds of food as the adults. They molt their skin 11 or 12 times before becoming fully grown. In winged species, the wing-buds appear in the last larval stage.

The females of other species incubate their eggs inside their bodies until they are ready to hatch. The Viviparous cockroach even produces live young.

# TERMITES

In a dry savannah in East Africa, giant termite mounds dominate the landscape. After a heavy storm, holes begin to appear in the sides of the mounds. Countless millions of winged male and female termites issue forth and take to the air for their mating flight. It is bonanza time for the spiders, ants, lizards, birds and small mammals, which gather to feast on the termites.

In many tropical countries, people join the feast, for they too eat termites. However, except for these annual swarms, termites are not often seen, for they live secretive lives, hidden in their nests.

Termites live in colonies and are truly social insects; the offspring of one generation help the parents in raising the next. Each colony consists of an egg-laying female or queen, and her mate, the king, both of which are winged and have good vision, and many wingless and usually blind workers and soldiers.

## SOCIAL COCKROACHES
Although termites are often called white ants, they are in fact closely related to cockroaches. The Darwin termite of Australia, for example, not only looks like the colonial Brown-hooded cockroach of North America, but it also contains in its gut the same

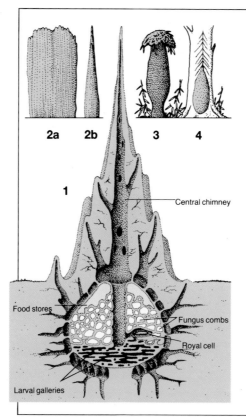

▲◀ **Termite mounds** A 20ft-tall mound of the Bellicose termite of Africa (1). Broadside and end-on view of mound of the Magnetic termite of Australia (2a,b). Nests of a soil-feeding termite (3) and of a tree termite (4).

▼▶ In the termite *Bellicositermes natalensis* the queen (1) and her dwarfed king (2) produce nymphs (3) from which other social classes, or castes, such as large soldiers (4), develop.

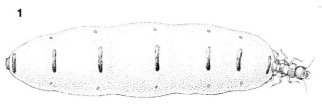

## TERMITES Order Isoptera
*(at least 2,230 species)*

 **Habitat:** mostly grassland.

**Diet:** plant material, including own cultivated fungi.

 **Relationship with people:** crop and timber pests, but also

beneficial by returning nutrients to soil.

**Distribution:** mostly in tropics.

**Size:** length ⅕-⅘in, some queens up to 5½in long.

**Color:** ranges from pearly white, straw, to dark brown.

**Species mentioned in text:**
Bellicose termite (*Macrotermes bellicosus*)

Darwin termite (*Mastotermes darwiniensis*)
Large termite (*Macrotermes subhyalinus*)
Magnetic termite (*Amitermes meridionalis*)
Snouted termites (*Hospitalitermes* species)
Toothed termites (*Odontotermes* species)
Tree termites (*Procubitermes* species)

species of microscopic single-celled animals (or protozoans), which help with the digestion of wood.

A termite colony begins when a winged male and female team up as a pair. They shed their wings and journey together to find a suitable nesting place. There, they mate and begin to rear young. The first larvae become workers. Their role is to feed the queen and king, to tend the eggs, and to build and repair the nests.

When there are enough workers to carry out all the routine tasks, the queen begins to rear soldiers. These protect the colony and columns of workers when they leave the nest in search of food.

Soldiers have either massively developed jaws for fighting off ants, which are their main enemies, or strange, pointed snouts. Those with snouts are called nasutes and they can squirt a jet of sticky liquid over a few inches. The liquid gums up, and may poison, attacking insects.

▲Grotesquely swollen, this queen Large termite lays up to 30,000 eggs a day.

◄A column of snouted termite workers forages on forest-floor lichens, guarded on both sides by nasute soldiers.

## WOOD- AND FUNGUS-EATERS

Many termites are major pests because they eat wood. The species that specialize in dry wood cause the most serious problems, often eating into structural timbers. Other wood-eating termites prefer damp, rotten wood. However, most species eat humus, soil, grass or leaves.

In dry parts of Africa and Asia, toothed and Large termites cultivate a special fungus in their nests on a network of combs made out of their droppings. The Termite fungus (*Termitomyces* species) is found only in the nests of these insects. It digests the droppings and the termites eat both the fungus and the comb.

# MANTIDS

In East Africa, a hoverfly lands on a flower in search of sweet nectar. The unsuspecting fly fails to notice that part of the flower is in fact a mantid. It pays with its life, for suddenly, the "flower" erupts, and the fly is trapped in the vice-like grip of two spiny legs. Once again, the mantid's resemblance to a flower has paid off.

Mantids are insect masters of the ambush attack. Their front legs are an armory of spines and hooks and they act like a hinged (gin) trap. They grab any insect that wanders within their reach, and bring the prey to their powerful toothed jaws.

### IN PRAYING POSITION
Lightning attack requires excellent eyesight, and mantids have large eyes set on the top of a triangular-shaped head. The eyes are sensitive to the slightest movement and the head is very mobile and swivels freely as the mantid's gaze follows a moving insect.

When a mantid waits for prey, it usually sits with its front legs raised, as if in prayer. This gave rise to the the popular name of Praying mantis for the Common mantid, which is found in Europe and North Africa.

### A LIFE OF STEALTH
Most mantid species live on trees and shrubs, while a number are found on the ground. Success as an ambush predator depends on not being seen by potential prey, and the mantids have many disguises.

The African flower mantid is pink, with fleshy outgrowths to the body that resemble the petals of flowers on which it sits. Several species are green and resemble a leaf in shape. The Crinkled leaf mantid of South America looks almost exactly like a crinkled leaf. It swings gently from side to side, as though blown by a gentle breeze.

While these disguises enable mantids to excel as surprise-attack hunters, they also protect mantids from falling prey themselves to lizards, birds and insect-eating mammals. If threatened, some species strike out with their spined forelegs to inflict a painful jab.

**MANTIDS** Order Mantodea
(*about 1,800 species*)

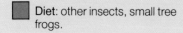
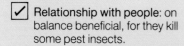

**Habitat:** mainly trees and shrubs in warmer countries, especially the tropics. A few ground-dwellers.

**Diet:** other insects, small tree frogs.

✓ **Relationship with people:** on balance beneficial, for they kill some pest insects.

**Distribution:** found in all the warmer parts of the world.

**Size:** length ⅖-6in.

**Color:** mostly drab green, gray or brown, resembling plant background; a few brightly colored flower mimics.

**Species mentioned in text:**
African flower mantid
(*Pseudocreobotra ocellata*)
Common European mantid (*Mantis religiosa*)
Crinkled leaf mantid (*Acanthops falcata*)
Grass mantids (*Polyspilota* species)
Mottled-green mantids (*Acontista* species)
Smaller leaf mantids (*Tithrone* species)
Stone-mimicking mantids
(*Eremiaphila* species)

▼ A stone-mimicking mantid takes advantage of its remarkable resemblance to a stone and seeks prey in the stony desert of the Arava Valley, southern Israel.

▲Poised for attack, a mottled-green mantid awaits prey on a flower in Trinidad. With the grasp of its front legs it can entrap an unwary insect in an instant.

▼A female grass mantid eats the head of a male while he continues to mate with her. A second male sits on her back while she continues her grisly meal.

## DEADLIER THAN THE MALE

Most people believe that a female mantid always eats her mate during copulation. But this is only partly true. In the smaller leaf mantids of South America, for example, cannibalism of this sort is never seen. In other species, it occurs in some instances.

Scientists now think that if a male mantid courts a female correctly, he is safe. If his courtship ritual is defective in some way, the female mistakes him for a prey species and eats him. By only mating with males that have courted her in the proper manner, and eating those which do not, a female mantid may ensure that her sons inherit the correct courtship behavior and therefore live to father many offspring of their own.

The males of many mantid species avoid being eaten by approaching the female carefully from behind and then leaping on to her back, out of reach of her front legs. Being smaller than the female, he is harder to grab in this position.

Female mantids lay between 10 and 400 eggs in a frothy mass called an ootheca, which soon hardens and dries in the air. It is usually attached to a stem, tree trunk or rock. Despite the protection of the ootheca, many mantid eggs are destroyed by the larvae of parasitic wasps.

# EARWIGS

In a small wood in southern France, two Common earwigs circle each other on a patch of bare, damp earth. One of them, a male, performs a little dance in front of the other one. He is courting a prospective mate. She accepts him by turning her back on him. Now the two insects mate – they place the ends of their abdomens in contact, with the male's uppermost.

During mating, earwigs grasp one another using the pair of pincers or forceps at the end of the abdomen. The pincers are the most characteristic feature of these familiar insects.

### APTLY NAMED?
Earwigs get their name from the age-old belief that they like to hide in people's ears, and it was feared that they would use the pincers to give a nasty nip. As with many folklore tales, there is an element of truth in this. Earwigs do like to creep about in small crevices, under loose bark or stones. Indeed, they are built for such a life, Their elongated slender bodies are smooth and flattened, they have short legs, and their chewing mouthparts are directed forwards on a flattened, highly mobile head.

It is also true that earwigs use their pincers in defense. If threatened, an earwig bends up the tip of its flexible abdomen into the air and brandishes its pincers in a threat display. But the pincers have other uses. In some species, they are thought to be used to open and fold the delicate hind wings. When at rest, these are kept in complicated folds and are protected by the short, leathery forewings, which are modified as wing cases, or elytra, rather as in beetles. Earwigs have also been seen to impale small insect prey on their pincers.

With the exception of the Small European earwig, those species living in cool countries rarely fly, and then only at night in hot weather. The Common earwig rarely flies, nevertheless it is now widespread in most parts of the world. This is the result of accidental transport of earwigs by people rather than the insect's own powers of locomotion.

### NOT FUSSY EATERS
Earwigs have a particularly varied diet. They use their biting and chewing mouthparts to eat mainly decaying plant and animal material and small live insects. They also feed on living plants, consuming especially flower buds, petals and fruit. When present in large numbers, the Common earwig becomes a serious garden pest.

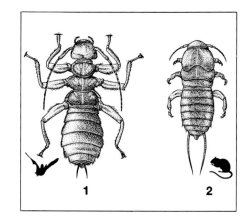

▲A bat earwig (1) from South-east Asia. Instead of being smooth and flattened, bat earwigs are robust and hairy and are about 1in long. They give birth to live young. A rat earwig (2) from South Africa. The short, hooked legs have pads on the feet, enabling the earwig to move freely through the rat's fur.

---

**EARWIGS** Order Dermaptera
(*about 1,200 species*)

 **Habitat:** mainly ground-dwellers in grassland and forests; often climb to tree canopy.

**Diet:** living and dead animal and plant material.

**Relationship with people:** mainly beneficial, disposing of dead material; sometimes pests of flowers.

**Distribution:** worldwide, except for polar regions.

**Size:** mostly slender, ⅖-2in long.

**Color:** rather drab; straw-colored to varying shades of brown.

**Species mentioned in text:**
Bat earwigs (*Arixenia* species)
Common earwig (*Forficula auricularia*)
Rat earwigs (*Hemimerus* species)
Small European earwig (*Labia minor*)

## MATERNAL CARE

In the tropics, earwigs mate and lay eggs all the year round. In cooler countries, they mate all year round, but egg-laying is restricted to the summer; the females store sperm for several months until it is needed.

Before she lays her eggs, a female earwig digs a short burrow in the soil. Into this she deposits 20 to 50 (depending on the species) pearly white, oval eggs. She remains in the burrow for 2 to 3 weeks until the eggs hatch. During this time, she cleans and turns the eggs regularly, keeping them free from fungal infection.

She guards her larvae against predators for a week or two, but then she tends to eat them. This encourages the larvae to leave the burrow and fend for themselves. The larvae molt four

▲This Common earwig is browsing on the ground among dead leaves, searching for small insects or rotting plant material.

◀A Common earwig sits in a mallow flower. Earwigs damage flowers by eating petals and chewing the pollen-bearing anthers.

or five times within about 2 months before they reach adulthood.

## STRANGE EARWIGS

In South-east Asia, there are two species of earwig that live in association with bats. They live either on the bats or in the caves where the bats roost. They feed on the bats' droppings and flakes of dead skin. Because bat earwigs live in total darkness, they have poor eyesight. They also lack wings, having no need to fly.

Equally strange are 10 species of South African earwig, which are true parasites. They live in the fur of Savannah giant pouched rats, where they feed on dead skin and the oily skin secretions of their hosts. Rat earwigs are blind and flightless.

# CRICKETS, GRASSHOPPERS

**A deafening chorus of insect sounds fills a summery meadow. Most of the songsters are grasshoppers and bush crickets and all of them are males. They sing in the hope of attracting females. Though easily heard, they remain largely unseen by enemies because they resemble their backgrounds so closely.**

## CRICKETS, GRASSHOPPERS Order
Orthoptera *(over 20,000 species)*

 **Habitat:** grasslands, desert, savannah, forest.

**Diet:** mainly stems, leaves, grasses, but some also eat insects.

 **Relationship with people:** species such as locusts are serious pests.

**Distribution:** worldwide, except polar regions and highest mountains.

**Size:** length ⅖-6in.

**Color:** black and browns, many mottled with gray, green, black and yellow; some blue and red.

**Species mentioned in text:**
Australian plague locust (*Chortoicetes terminifera*)
Desert locust (*Schistocerca gregaria*)
Dying leaf bush cricket (*Pycnopalpa bicordata*)
European field cricket (*Gryllus campestris*)
European house cricket (*Acheta domestica*)
European mole cricket (*Gryllotalpa vinae*)
Golden-horned grasshopper (*Taenipoda auricornis*)
Great green bush cricket (*Tettigonia viridissima*)
Migratory locust (*Locusta migratoria*)
Mottled stone grasshopper (*Oedipoda miniata*)

Crickets and grasshoppers are among the most successful of all insects. They live in most parts of the world, especially in warm places.

The familiar grasshoppers of fields and dry waste ground belong to the short-horned grasshoppers. Their antennae have less than 30 segments, and the long, muscular hind legs are built for leaping. Most species have well-developed wings and can fly in hot weather.

The long-horned grasshoppers all have more than 30 segments in each antenna. They are usually called bush crickets, or, in North America, katydids. They, too, have long hind legs, but are not such powerful leapers as the grasshoppers.

The true crickets are nocturnal and spend their days in burrows in the soil or under stones and logs.

## FOOD AND FEEDING
Grasshoppers and crickets have biting and chewing mouthparts and their jaws are very strong. Most species eat living plant material, including stems, but especially leaves and grasses.

When feeding, a grasshopper rests so that it straddles both sides of the leaf. This means that its jaws can get a direct grip on the leaf edge, rather like scissors on paper.

Bush crickets, when feeding, may stand on only four of their six legs. This frees the front pair of legs to handle pieces of bitten-off leaf so that either the sensitive palps can inspect them or they can hold them while the jaws chew away.

Many bush crickets are omnivorous and eat other insects as well as plant material. The European house cricket even eats cloth and paper. In some parts of the world, people use crickets

▼A larva of the Golden-horned grasshopper eats a cactus fruit in a Mexican desert. Cactus fruits are an important source of water for this desert grasshopper. This larva's developing wings are clearly visible.

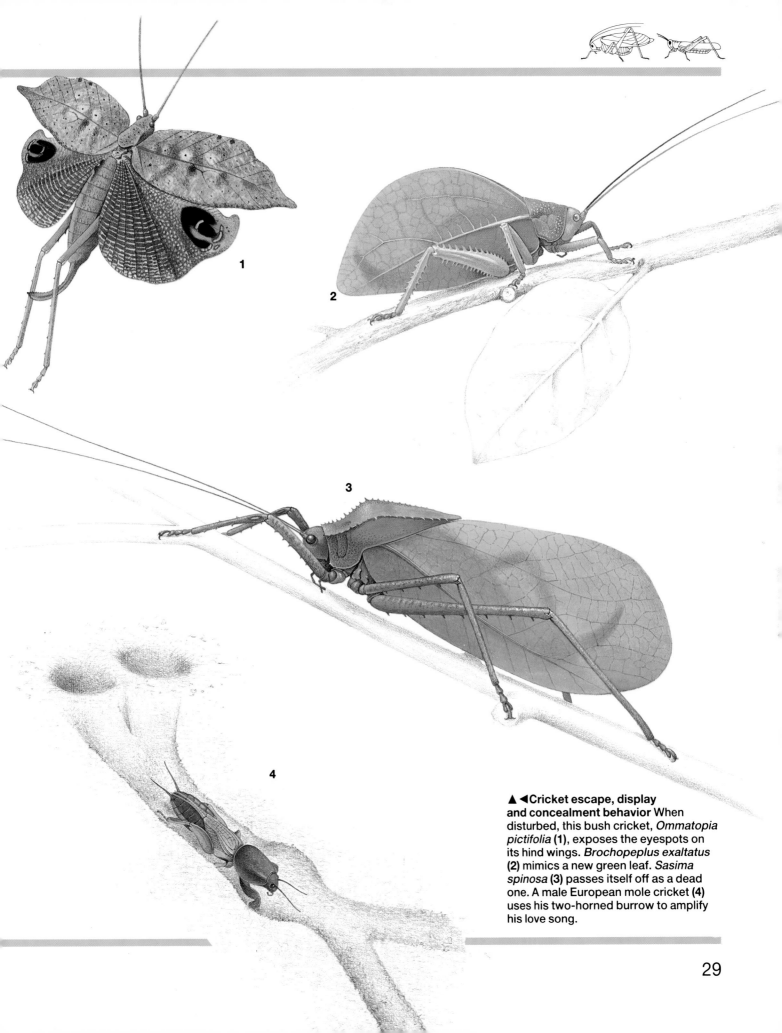

▲ ◄ **Cricket escape, display and concealment behavior** When disturbed, this bush cricket, *Ommatopia pictifolia* (**1**), exposes the eyespots on its hind wings. *Brochopeplus exaltatus* (**2**) mimics a new green leaf. *Sasima spinosa* (**3**) passes itself off as a dead one. A male European mole cricket (**4**) uses his two-horned burrow to amplify his love song.

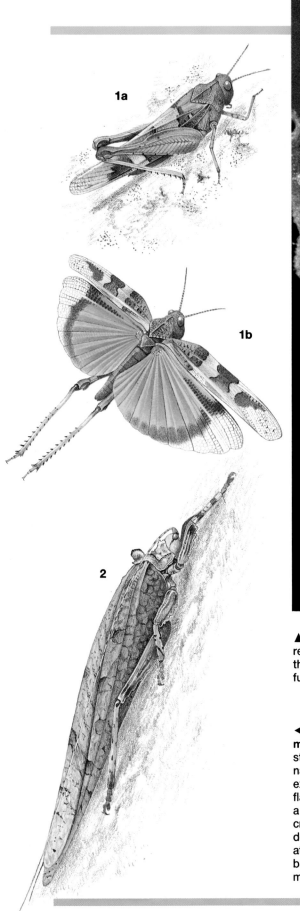

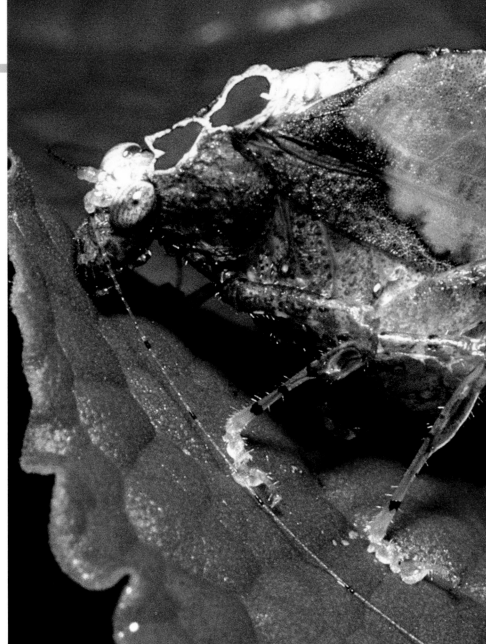

▲This Dying leaf bush cricket is a remarkable mimic of a freshly fallen leaf that has suffered damage by insects and fungal disease.

◄Grasshopper display and lichen-mimic At rest, the European Mottled stone grasshopper (1a) resembles its namesake, but if disturbed (1b) it exposes brightly colored hind wings in a flash display, which startles and deters a hungry bird. This Malaysian bush cricket (*Acanthodes* species) (2) lives in deep forest, where it is protected from attack by resembling the lichen-covered bark on which it rests motionless during much of the day.

as living corn removers; the insects' powerful jaws are good at removing horny skin from feet and toes.

## INSECT SONGSTERS
The success of crickets and grasshoppers is tied up with their ability to be heard, but not seen. Males use their "calling" song, each unique to their kind, to attract mates of the correct species. The males of territorial species have a different song to mark out their areas. A male defends his territory with a burst of "aggressive" singing when a neighboring male looks set to invade his patch.

## RASPS AND EARS ON LEGS

Grasshoppers make sounds in a way totally different from bush crickets. They rub small, peg-like projections on the inner face of the upper part (femur) of each hind leg against a specially hardened vein on the forewings. This is known as stridulation. There are a few species in which the females stridulate, but their efforts are feeble compared with the males.

Both the European field and house crickets have attractive songs and are sometimes kept as pets.

The ears of a grasshopper are positioned one on either side of the first abdominal segment. Each consists of a thin membrane, the back of which is connected to special nerve cells. Sound waves make the membrane vibrate and this stimulates the nerve cells so that the insect "hears."

The ears of bush crickets, true crickets and mole crickets work in the same way, but they are located on the front legs rather than the abdomen.

## MATING AND EGG-LAYING

When a male cricket or grasshopper has attracted a female to his patch, he may, according to species, leap on her and mate immediately, or he may perform a further courtship. This can be a display of special body markings or a dance involving special leg and body movements.

Mating may last several hours. Afterwards, the female begins to lay her eggs. Female bush crickets have a blade-like egg-laying tube (ovipositor) and usually deposit eggs singly, either in plant tissue or in rough bark.

Female grasshoppers do not have a conspicuous ovipositor and they lay eggs in batches of 10 to 200, often deep in the soil, and surrounded by a protective foam. The female uses her short, pronged ovipositor to burrow. Special muscles between the body segments allow her to extend her abdomen down to more than twice its normal length before laying her eggs.

Most males accept the rights of a territory holder and fights are rare. By behaving in this way, the males of territorial species become more or less evenly spaced in the field and each individual increases his chances of attracting females.

The communication system used by grasshoppers and crickets requires the ability not only to make very special noises, but also the ability to hear and understand them.

The males of true crickets and bush crickets produce their songs by rubbing together specialized areas at the base of the wings. The songs of many bush crickets are almost inaudible to the human ear. The Great green bush cricket of Europe is an exception. Its persistent song on a late summer evening carries a long way and sounds just like a bicycle free-wheeling fast downhill.

The European mole cricket has no difficulty in making itself heard. The males sing from within a specially excavated burrow in the soil that branches into two before reaching the surface. This structure amplifies the sound so well that a calling male may be heard, and readily located, on a still evening from up to 1¼mi away.

The eggs hatch to produce larvae, which are miniature versions of the adults, although they have no wings. The larvae molt from three to five times before becoming adults. The length of the larval period depends on the species and local conditions.

**DEFENSE**
A juicy grasshopper or bush cricket makes a nice meal for a lizard or bird. Thus, while it is important for most grasshoppers and crickets to make themselves heard, they must also make it difficult to be seen.

▼ Desert locusts in Africa congregate on the upper branches of a shrub to absorb the warmth of the early morning sun.

Most species accomplish this by blending in with their surroundings. This camouflage adaptation explains the astonishing diversity of form to be found among grasshoppers and crickets. Many desert species look like stones, forest dwellers often resemble lichen-covered bark, and a number of species are very convincing mimics of leaves.

Among the leaf mimics, camouflage reaches extremes. They mimic not only a leaf's shape and color, but also its pattern of veins and even blotches of damage by fungi and insects.

If they are disturbed, many camouflaged species, such as the Mottled stone grasshopper of Europe and Asia, leap and fly away with a flash

exposure of bright color on the hind wings. This startles a predator.

If the worst comes to the worst and a bird manages to grasp a grasshopper by its leg, it can shed the leg and escape, similar to a lizard shedding its tail under similar circumstances.

Another line of defense involves bold advertizing rather than camouflage. Many grasshoppers are brightly colored and they feed in the open on poisonous plants. The plants evolved the poisons to deter grazing animals, but the grasshoppers are unaffected by these chemicals. Indeed, they store them in their bodies. Birds and other predators learn to associate the bright colors of the grasshoppers with a vile taste and avoid the insects.

▲ Australian plague locusts eat their way through a meadow. They are a major pest to pasture and crops.

▼ A swarm of Australian plague locusts in a field of alfalfa (lucerne) makes the going difficult for this farmer.

## A PLAGUE OF LOCUSTS

The two most famous locusts are the Desert locust and Migratory locust, both of which live mainly in the arid areas of Africa and the Middle East. But there are locusts also in North and South America, Asia and Australia.

Locusts are no different from the other short-horned grasshoppers, except that they exist in two different forms: solitary and gregarious.

The solitary form lives just like an ordinary grasshopper, feeding on the sparse vegetation in desert and semi-desert areas. It is drab-colored and blends in well with its background.

After some rain, things begin to change. The plant growth becomes more lush, and with more food the female grasshoppers lay more eggs. But the most dramatic change is in the behavior and appearance of the new generation of larval grasshoppers. Instead of carrying on a solitary life, they band together in huge groups. And instead of being drab and dull, they develop striking color patterns of yellow, black and orange.

As the rains continue, the hoppers feed and many bands join up, so that the area becomes swamped with millions of hoppers on the march.

The larvae molt for a fifth and final time and become adult. They fly to food in the mornings and evenings. During the day, they roost in countless numbers on trees and shrubs. Eventually, they eat all of the available green leaves and grasses. The hungry grasshoppers take to the wing in search of new feeding grounds – a locust swarm is born.

### ON THE MOVE

A locust swarm may contain over 500 million locusts per sq mi, and cover 400sq mi. This is at least 50,000 million locusts weighing over 70,000 tons. Each day, such a swarm eats nearly four times the weight of food eaten by people in London or New York City. The swarm flies downwind until it finds a new patch of green vegetation. All too often, this is a crop, such as millet, on which people depend. The locusts are dreaded because they can destroy a crop in a few hours. In 1957, a swarm of Desert locusts consumed some 185,000 tons of grain in Africa, sufficient to feed 1 million people for a year.

Usually, the swarm flies southwards, behind weather fronts. This means that the locusts follow the pattern of rainfall and always have fresh green plants on which to feed. Sometimes, though, if farmers are lucky, the winds blow the locusts out to sea and the exhausted swarm will fall from the sky and drown.

The Migratory locust is capable of flying much greater distances than the Desert locust and, in a warm summer, sometimes reaches southern Europe and even the British Isles. Recently, it has managed to cross the Atlantic and has been found on some of the Caribbean islands.

Back in the area where the swarm first appeared, the rains stop and the few larvae to emerge from the nearly dried-out egg pods develop not as brightly colored, gregarious locusts, but as drab, solitary grasshoppers.

33

# STICK AND LEAF INSECTS

Eyes aswivel, a chameleon makes its way slowly along a branch in southern Spain. Occasionally, it stops and, with a lightening flick of its long, sticky tongue, catches an unwary insect. Naturally, it ignores a green offshoot of a nearby branch. Even the chameleon's excellent eyesight fails to spot that the offshoot is in fact a green form of the French stick insect.

This kind of successful escape story is repeated millions of times a day in warm countries all over the world. Stick and leaf insects are masters of some of the best disguises found among insects. These animals are surrounded by hungry enemies and have arrived at many ingenious ways to avoid being eaten by meat-eating lizards, birds and the like. One of the best forms of self defense is to look like, or mimic, something inedible.

## NIGHT-TIME MUNCHERS
As their names imply, stick and leaf insects resemble sticks, twigs and leaves. These distant relatives of the crickets and grasshoppers have biting and chewing mouthparts. They feed at night on leaves and green stems. During the day, they remain nearly motionless for hours on end.

Stick and leaf insects have thread-like antennae and small eyes. Many species of stick insect lack wings and are flightless. In other species, usually only the males are winged and they can fly short distances. The longest of all insects is the Saw-footed stick insect of South-east Asia, which can reach a length of 13in. Smaller species are often kept as pets. They are easy to look after and breed.

## ABLE TO DECEIVE
Stick insects are all long and thin, with the mid-section of the body greatly extended. Many species have sharp outgrowths that look like thorns, and some also have small nodules that could be mistaken for plant leaf buds. Others, such as the Giant Australian stick insect, have leafy outgrowths to the body and legs as well as a fierce array of spines and thorns. These additional structures, together with their drab gray or dark green color, heighten the stick insects' remarkable resemblance to inedible twigs.

## WALKING LEAVES
While stick insects have a very wide distribution, leaf insects, are restricted to South-east Asia. Their resemblance to leaves is superb. The forewings in males and the abdomen in both sexes are greatly expanded. These structures often have crinkly edges, and the insects have what appears to be a midrib and system of veins, like a real leaf. The legs also have leaf-like flaps.

**STICK AND LEAF INSECTS** Order Phasmatoidea (or Phasmida) (*Over 2,500 species*)

Habitat: grassland, scrub, forest.

Diet: leaves and green stems.

Relationship with people: occasionally pests of eucalyptus forests in Australia.

Distribution: worldwide in warmer areas; leaf insects restricted to South-east Asia, New Guinea, Australia.

Size: length up to 13in.

Color: gray, green, brown, often blotched to resemble fungal or insect damage.

Species mentioned in text:
French stick insect (*Clonopsis gallicus*)
Giant Australian stick insect (*Extatosoma tiaratum*)
Laboratory stick insect (*Caraursius morosus*)
Leaf insects (*Phyllium* species)
Saw-footed stick insect (*Pharnacia serratipes*)

◄This Venezuelan stick insect avoids attack by resembling the lichen-covered bark and leaves on which it rests. The outgrowths from the insect's body blur its outline.

As with stick insects, the mimicry effect is much improved by color. Leaf insects are either a pale, fresh-leaf green, resembling a new leaf, or a drab dark green or brown, resembling a dead or dying leaf. This variation in color can be found within a population of the same species.

The whole effect is of a flat cluster of leaves. In fact, the resemblance is so good that occasionally an inquisitive herbivore, such as a deer, may nibble at a leaf insect. Evidently, the risk of this happening is outweighed by the advantage of looking like a leaf and thereby avoiding the attentions of the many insect-eating birds.

## SEVERAL LINES OF DEFENSE
We might think that mimicking a twig or leaf is sufficient protection. In the battle to remain alive, however, these insects have many more defensive tricks in their armory.

Stick insects not only resemble the twigs they rest on, but they have just the right surface texture, so that they "feel" like a twig. Leaf insects, too, have a leafy texture.

The world of twigs and leaves is not uniform. Some leaves, for example, may be damaged by insects. Others will be blotched with fungal growths. Many species of leaf insect also have markings that resemble the symptoms of attack by other plant pests, such as bacteria and viruses.

It is no use looking like a stick or a leaf if you do not behave like one. This is why these insects are slow movers and spend much of their time perfectly still. But plants are not motionless. Thus, many stick insects, and all of the leaf insects, sway slightly from side to side, just like a twig or leaf caught in a gentle breeze.

◄A leaf insect in New Guinea, looking like a dead, crinkled leaf with fungal growths. Other species are green and resemble fresh, new leaves.

The accuracy with which stick, and particularly leaf, insects resemble the parts of plants is a direct result of the good eyesight of insect-eating lizards and birds. The better the eyesight of the predator, the closer the protective resemblance to inedible objects has to be if the insect is continually to survive detection.

**FAIL-SAFE PROTECTION**
No matter how good the resemblance of these insects to their backgrounds, there will always be the occasional extra-alert lizard or bird that can spot such prey and attempt to turn them, one at a time, into a meal.

If its disguise fails in this way, the stick or leaf insect has further protective devices to avoid being eaten. The commonest among stick insects is to feign death when attacked. The insect falls to the ground or a lower branch and lies perfectly still. Once again, it becomes difficult to see, and the bird usually gives up and searches for food elsewhere in the branches.

Stick insects with wings have yet another line of defense. If attacked, some species suddenly open their fan like hind wings and display a blotch of bright color. The sudden display of such a brilliant color by an otherwise drab insect startles the would-be predator and frightens it away. Other species use their wings to create a sudden rustling noise, with the same effects.

**CHEMICAL PROTECTION**
Some stick insects have glands in the front of the body that squirt out a foul-smelling, vile-tasting froth if the insect is attacked. Yet others simply regurgitate the contents of their gut over the predator – a clear invitation to leave the stick insect alone.

Among South American stick insects, some give off a foul smell which may protect them from attack by army ants. These fearsome predators prey on various small animals in the rain forest. They hunt in vast, marching columns, and often walk over stick insects hiding motionless in the vegetation, without harming them.

Although well protected from any attack, stick and leaf insects do have some successful enemies. Females of several species of parasitic fly lay their eggs on them. The fly larvae burrow inside the stick or leaf insect and eat it, eventually killing it.

**AN ABSENCE OF MALES**
Adult stick insects are usually widely spaced among the vegetation and, although males can usually fly, there is always a danger that mating will not take place. Female stick insects overcome this by being able to lay eggs that develop without being fertilized. This is called parthenogenesis. In some species, such as the Laboratory stick insect, which is often kept in schools, males are unknown and reproduction by parthenogenesis is the only way to increase numbers.

Female stick and leaf insects lay eggs one at a time and usually drop them from their abdomens wherever they happen to be. However, some female stick insects flick the egg for some distance by jerking the tip of the abdomen. The egg has a very tough skin and resembles a seed, so much so that harvester ants, which gather seeds, may carry them back to their nest for food.

**A COLORFUL BEGINNING**
Each egg hatches to produce a larva which is a miniature version of the adult. Males must undergo five molts before becoming adult, while females molt six times. The larvae of some species are very different from the adult in that they are brightly colored in such a way as to suggest to predators that they may be distasteful.

Although stick and leaf insects are normally solitary creatures, several species in Australia do cause serious leaf-loss in eucalyptus forests.

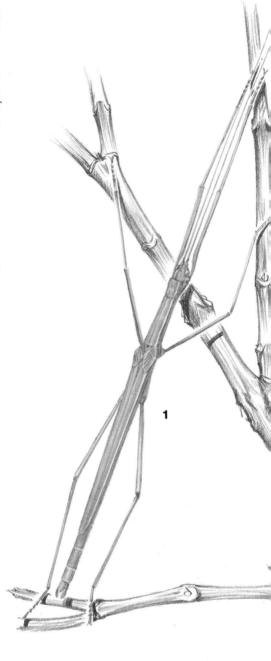

▲▶ **Stick insects from around the world** A species of *Necroscia* (1), from Malaysia. *Acanthoclonia paradoxa* (2), from Trinidad, is so stick-like it can sit safely on leaves in full view, like a fallen twig. *Acrophylla titan* (3), is the longest in Australia, sometimes reaching 10in. A South American species of *Stratoctes* (4), from Peru. A female of the Giant Australian stick insect (*Extatosoma tiaratum*) (5).

# LICE

**The classroom is quiet as the children sit with heads bent over their work. The heads of two of the children touch as they are engrossed in their drawing. Unseen and unsuspected, a head louse moves from the hair of one child to the other's. In a week, the sound of scratching crayons will be joined by the sound of scratching children as the infestation of head lice spreads.**

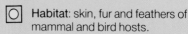    

**LICE** Order Phthiraptera
(*about 3,150 species*)

Habitat: skin, fur and feathers of mammal and bird hosts.

Diet: flakes of skin and feathers, blood, and skin oils and waxes.

Relationship with people: harmful; can transmit typhus and relapsing fever.

Distribution: worldwide.

Size: length 1/5-2/5in.

Color: gray to brown, often red after blood meal in transparent species.

Species mentioned in text:
Dog louse (*Trichodectes canis*)
Guinea pig louse (*Gliricola porcelli*)
Human body louse (*Pediculis humanus*)
Human crab louse (*Phthirus pubis*)
Human head louse (*Pediculis capitis*)

In much of Europe, head lice are a frequent problem in schools. Over the years, they have become resistant to many insecticide shampoos.

Lice are true parasites. They are wingless and spend their entire lives living on the skin or among the feathers or fur of their bird or mammal hosts. It is likely that lice evolved from insect scavengers in the nests of early mammals and birds, feeding on skin and feather debris.

## HANGING ON TO THEIR HOSTS

There are two main kinds of lice: sucking and biting. Sucking lice include the three species that live on people – the Head louse, Body louse and Crab louse. These all pierce the skin with their mouthparts and suck blood. They have little pouches in their gut that contain bacteria and yeasts that help with the digestion of the blood.

Like all lice, human lice have flattened bodies. The legs are short and curved, and each is armed at the tip with claws that enable the insects to grasp the hairs of the host animal.

Infestations of human lice are most frequent where people live in poor, overcrowded conditions. But lice do not require dirty conditions. They become a problem in any place where many people come into close contact with one another.

The Head louse and the Body louse are closely related species and resemble each other. The Crab louse belongs to a separate genus, and is very different in appearance. As its name suggests, it is squat in shape, and broader than long. Its claws are more robust, for it lives among the coarser, thicker pubic hairs of the groin.

During the course of her life, a female Body louse lays up to 250 eggs. These hatch after 8 or 9 days and the new larvae take a blood meal immediately. A single female can give rise to up to 15,000 female descendents in about 80 days. The heaviest recorded count of Body lice on a single person was 3,800. The record for Head lice on a single person is 1,434. The eggs of the Head louse appear as silvery specks in the hair and are called nits.

## CEMENTED ON

The biting lice live on birds or mammals. Some, like the Dog louse, use their jaws to make wounds and feed on blood. Others, for example the Guinea pig (Pet cavy) louse, feed on oils from the hosts' hair follicles. Most bird lice feed on feathers.

The females of all biting lice glue their eggs singly to the hairs or feathers of the host with a quick-drying cement. This cement resists water and therefore the eggs cannot be removed by washing.

▲A recent blood meal shows dark red inside the body of this larva of a Human head louse. Just visible are the claws for hanging on to the person's hairs.

## LICE AND HUMAN DISEASES

The Head and Crab lice do not spread any diseases, although heavy infestations may result in skin infections because of frantic scratching by the host. The Body louse, though, is notorious because it spreads typhus and relapsing fever from infected persons to new hosts. Typhus killed 3 million people in Eastern Europe during World War I.

◀Lice cannot live separately from their hosts. If the host dies, so do the lice as the host's body cools. However, some birds, such as this young swift, are infested with parasitic flies called louse-flies. Lice sometimes hitch a lift to another host by grasping the bristles of these flies. A louse-fly acts as an unsuspecting "flying lifeboat." However, louse-flies are not as choosy about hosts as the lice, and the hitch-hikers may end up on the wrong host and die.

▼An adult female Human head louse magnified 80 times. The five-segmented antennae are sensitive to touch, smell and temperature. Males are about half this size.

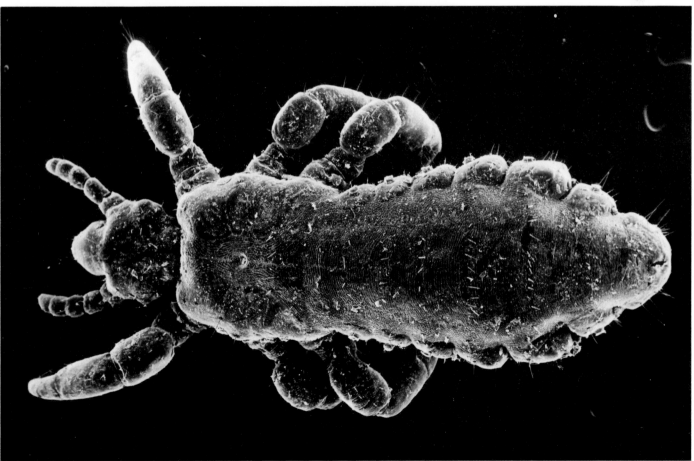

# BUGS

Hundreds of greenflies cluster along a stem of meadowsweet. Most of the soft-bodied insects sit still, with their mouthparts sunk into the stem, taking up sap. A few walk about slowly, occasionally probing the stem, while some large females give birth to live young. And all the time, Red ants tend the greenflies, drinking droplets of sweet honeydew emerging from their abdomens.

Meadowsweet greenflies or aphids benefit from the ants' attentions. In return for the honeydew, the ants drive away all ladybirds and hoverfly larvae that would eat the aphids.

Greenflies belong to a group of insects commonly called bugs. All bugs have piercing and sucking mouthparts called the rostrum or beak. This enables bugs to get at and suck up a range of liquid food. In the case of aphids, the rostrum penetrates the tissues of the plant through which sap flows.

## VARIATIONS IN FORM

There are two major groups of bug. The larger is the Homoptera. This includes the aphids and comprises plant-suckers in which both the fore- and hind wings are membranous and similar in size and shape. The rostrum is hinged downwards for feeding, never forwards, and at rest the wings slope over the body. The Homoptera also includes the leafhoppers, froghoppers, cicadas and scale insects.

In the other group, the Heteroptera, the base of the forewings is thickened and leathery. The remainder of the forewings and the hind wings are membranous. At rest, the wings overlap and lie flat over the body. The rostrum can be swung down or forwards for feeding. The Heteroptera include the shieldbugs, the assassin

---

**BUGS** Order Hemiptera
*(at least 67,500 species)*

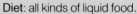 **Habitat**: mainly grassland, forest and scrub.

**Diet**: all kinds of liquid food.

**Relationship with people**: many crop pests, transmitters of plant diseases. Some bloodsuckers attack humans and spread disease; some beneficial, kill insect pests.

**Distribution**: almost worldwide.

**Size**: body length 1/50-3in.

**Color**: many mottled gray-brown and camouflaged; others green or with bright warning colors.

**Species mentioned in text**:
Australian gum cicada (*Venustria superba*)
Bedbug (*Cimex lectularius*)
Bee-killer assassin bug (*Pristhesanchus papuensis*)
Black bean aphid (*Aphis fabae*)
Hawthorn shieldbug (*Acanthosoma haemorrhoidalis*)
Meadowsweet aphid (*Macrosiphum cholodkovskyi*)
Parent shieldbug (*Elasmucha grisea*)
Paternal assassin bug (*Rhinocoris tristis*)
Peach aphid (*Myzus persicae*)
Rose aphid (*Macrosiphum rosae*)

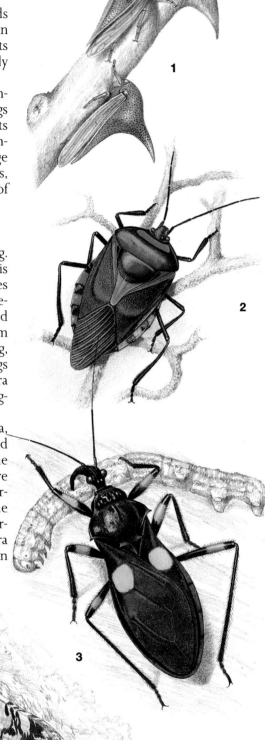

1

2

3

4

**◄▼Bugs in several habitats**
Treehoppers (*Umbonia spinosa*) **(1)**, resembling thorns. This shieldbug *Catacanthus anchorago* **(2)**, has a warning coloration. An assassin bug, *Acanthaspis* species **(3)**, feeds on the body fluids of a caterpillar. This mottled lanternfly *Phenax variegata* **(4)**, resembles lichen-covered bark. The surface film of water is home to the Water strider (*Hydrometra stagnorum*) **(5)**, and the Pond skater (*Gerris lacustris*) **(6)**. The Saucer bug (*Ilyocoris cimicioides*) **(7)** hunts under water. The Water scorpion (*Nepa cinerea*) **(8)**, breathes through its respiratory siphon. The Water boatman (*Corixa punctata*) **(9)**, uses its hind legs as paddles, as does the backswimmer (*Notonecta glauca*) **(10)**. The Water stick insect (*Ranatra linearis*) **(11)**, catches a tadpole with its front legs.

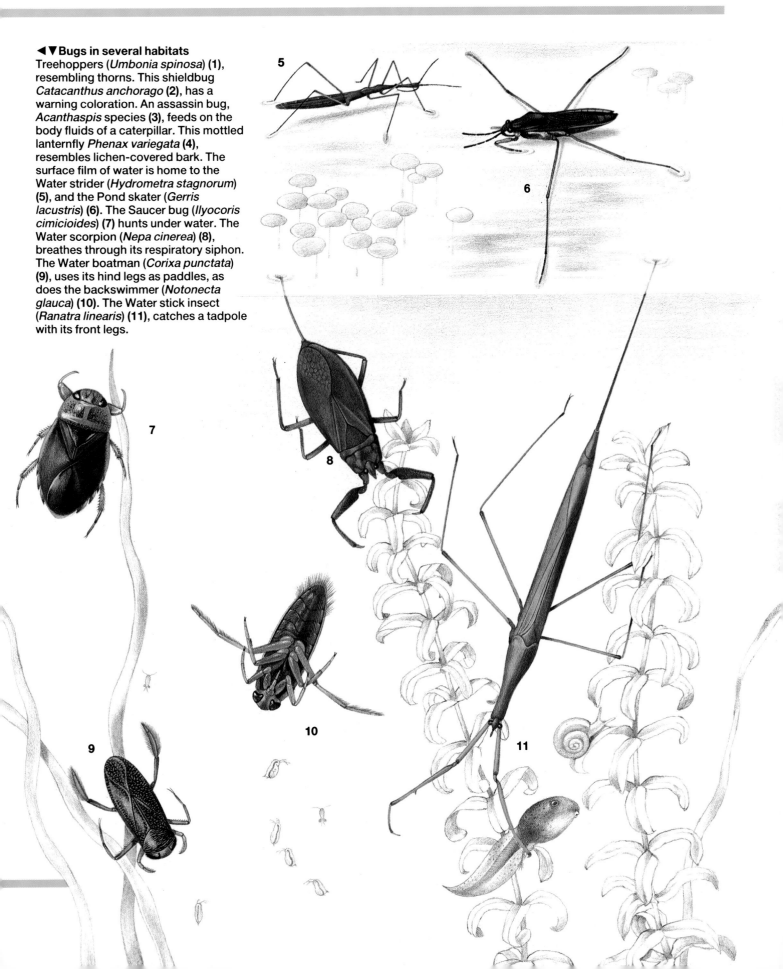

bugs, all the water bugs, the bedbug and the leaf or capsid bugs. All species have special glands in the thorax that give off a very unpleasant smell. Indeed, the shieldbugs are frequently called stinkbugs because of this.

Heteroptera are often very brightly colored and in such a way that they signal to would-be predators, such as birds, that they are distasteful. Young birds soon learn that such coloration is associated with a nasty experience.

**BLOOD-SUCKERS AND KILLERS**
Although many of the Heteroptera suck plant fluids, several kinds, for

example the assassin bugs and water bugs, have become predators. They suck the body fluids of other insects. A few have become bloodsuckers and attack reptiles, birds and mammals.

Some species such as the Hawthorn shieldbug, which feeds on hawthorn berries, use their rostrum to inject digestive juices into their food. This liquifies it so that it can be sucked up. Assassin bugs do the same with their insect prey and can often be seen carrying their victims impaled on the rostrum. One species, the Bee-killer assassin bug of Australia and New Guinea, awaits it prey at flowers.

▲ A newly hatched adult cicada emerges from its larval skin on a gum tree in Australia. The wings will soon expand and harden, and the cicada will develop its mottled camouflage pattern.

**LOVE SONGS**
The song of male cicadas is a familiar and often penetrating sound in summer in warm countries. Each species has its own characteristic song, and the male sings in order to attract a female with which it can mate. The females are silent.

Unlike grasshoppers, male cicadas do not produce sound by rubbing together parts of the body. Instead, they use a pair of thin membranes in their hard outer casing, the cuticle, on either side of the base of the abdomen. Each membrane, or tymbal, is distorted or buckled by a large muscle, rather like a tin-lid being clicked in and out. Each tug of the muscle produces a click or pulse of sound. Some species produce 1,000 pulses per second; each cicada's song consists of a distinctive sequence of pulses. The sounds are amplified by large air sacs in the abdomen. The human ear can hear the insects' songs from up to 1,200yd away.

After mating, female cicadas lay eggs in woody stems of trees and shrubs. On hatching, the larvae drop to the ground, where they develop.

## COMPLICATED LIVES
The larvae of most bugs molt six times before they become adult. During growth, there may be changes in the shape of the head and body. There is no pupal stage, and the larvae usually feed on similar food to the adults.

Many aphids have a more complicated life cycle, often involving several generations each year. These differ from one another in appearance and behavior. Thus, the Black bean aphid has one generation a year that has both males and females, and which therefore reproduces sexually. The females lay eggs on Spindle trees, where they pass the winter. The eggs hatch in spring as a generation of wingless females that reproduce without mating (parthenogenesis). They give birth to live young.

After two or three such asexual generations, a generation of winged females is produced. These develop on the Spindle trees, but in May they migrate to Field bean plants, where they, in turn, give birth to live young without mating. This new generation also gives birth to live young, but this time the offspring have wings. The young aphids migrate in autumn back to Spindle trees, where they all give

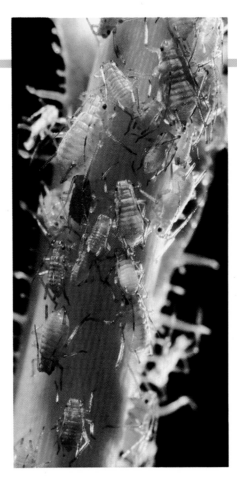

birth to live young, both males and females. These mate and the females then lay eggs. The year's cycle is now complete.

## PARENTAL CARE
Most female bugs have nothing more to do with their offspring once they have laid their eggs. However, a few species do look after their young. A female of the Parent shieldbug of Europe guards her clutch for 2 to 3 weeks and then remains with the larvae until they have passed through their second molt.

With some bugs, it is the males that look after the eggs. With females of the giant water bugs of the tropics each glues a batch of eggs on the back of its mate immediately after mating. The eggs remain attached to their father until they hatch. In Africa, it is the male of the Paternal assassin bug that guards the egg batch laid by his mate. He chases away small parasitic wasps that try to lay their eggs inside those of the female bug.

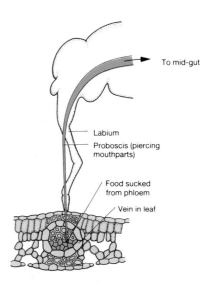

◀▲Rose aphids cluster around a rose stem (left). The rostrum of an aphid (above) penetrates a plant vein. It is an elongated tube made up of four threads, or stylets, enclosed in a tubular labium. Within the rostrum, one groove acts as a channel for injecting saliva, the other as a channel for sucking up liquid food.

## PEST BUGS
A heavy infestation of aphids can cause serious damage to a crop by making the plants wilt. More serious, though, is the spread of disease. The Peach aphid alone spreads 108 different types of virus that attack plants. Feeding holes in cotton bolls made by cotton stainer bugs allow a fungus to invade the cotton and make it useless.

In South America, there are blood-sucking assassin bugs that spread human disease. Their bites transmit a blood parasite from person to person, often with fatal results. More widespread is the bedbug. This lives in crevices in houses, and while people sleep at night, it sucks their blood. It was once common in overcrowded accommodation in poor areas. The bite of the bedbug causes pain and itching, and the wound may occasionally become infected by scratching. The bedbug's relatives include species that live in caves and attack bats; its association with humans may date from our cave-dwelling ancestors.

# BEETLES

A fly basks in a sheltered hollow between sand dunes. The insect is doomed, for it has been spotted by a tiger beetle. When the beetle gets to within 3in of the fly, it makes a lightning pounce. In an instant, the fly is dead, as the tiger beetle skewers it on its massive, five-toothed jaws.

Tiger beetles are the fastest insects in the world. These active and voracious hunters specialize in the sudden dash attack, and can run at speeds of up to 24in a second.

Speed is not the only secret of the tiger beetle's success. It has large, forward-looking eyes that can sense the slightest movement. Also, it can fly. Together, acute vision and lightning speed make all species of tiger beetle awesome hunting machines.

### THE BEETLE ERA
Success is the hallmark of beetles in general. They are everywhere, and they account for almost one-third of all described animal species, that is, more than 300,000 species. One family alone, the weevils, has 60,000 species. By comparison, there are only about 4,500 mammal species. If the Cretaceous period was the Age of Dinosaurs, then today we are living through the Age of the Beetles.

All beetles have biting and chewing mouthparts and they have independently evolved structures found also in earwigs and some bugs: the horny elytra, or wing cases. These are the modified front pair of wings. The elytra are raised in flight and may provide some lift, but the task of flying is performed by the hind wings.

At rest, the hind wings are thrown into complicated folds and tucked

▶ These mating leaf beetles from Peru are protected by their bright warning coloration. Birds learn to associate these color patterns with a nasty taste.

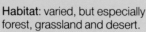

**BEETLES** Order Coleoptera
(*at least 300,000 species*)

**Habitat:** varied, but especially forest, grassland and desert.

**Diet:** mostly plant-feeders or predators, but many omnivores.

**Relationship with people:** many beneficial species and many serious pests of crops.

**Distribution:** almost everywhere.

**Size:** length 1/100-8in.

**Color:** from black, to bright metallic silver, green or blue. Many with warning coloration, others drab and camouflaged.

**Species mentioned in text:**
Bark beetles (*Scolytus* species)
Bark timber beetle (*Onychocerus crassus*)
Bombardier beetles (*Brachinus* species)
Burying beetles (*Nicrophorus* species)
Clover weevil (*Sitona sulcifrons*)
Deathwatch beetle (*Xestobium rufovillosum*)
European diving beetle (*Dytiscus marginalis*)
Fireflies (*Photinus* species)
Flower chafers (*Amphicoma* species)
Giant fungus beetle (*Pselaphicus giganteus*)
Nut weevil (*Curculio nucum*)
Oak longhorn (*Rhagium sycophanta*)
Oil beetles (*Mylabris* species)
Predatory fireflies (*Photurus* species)
Seed beetles (*Endustomus* species)
Seven-spot ladybird (*Coccinella septempunctata*)
Soldier beetle (*Rhagonycha fulva*)
Stag beetle (*Lucanus cervus*)
Tiger beetles (*Cicindela* species)
Tortoise beetles (*Omaspides* species)
Viviparous leaf beetle (*Eugonycha* species)

beneath the elytra, which meet in the middle. The elytra protect the hind wings and also provide a tough shield for the abdomen.

### SPECIALIST FEEDERS
Beetles have evolved an astonishing range of life-styles and feeding habits. Some eat and dispose of dead wood. Others perform the same service with the bodies of dead animals. Many beetles eat leaves, while some hunt insect prey under water, where they spend the whole of their lives. Several species rummage for food in leaf litter or burrow in the soil.

▲A European diving beetle awaits passing prey. The fringe of hairs on the hind legs makes them more efficient paddles for swimming.

▶Mating Soldier beetles, a common sight in summer in Europe. Their name harks back to the days when English soldiers wore red tunics.

Species such as the flower chafers of the eastern Mediterranean area, are the main pollinators of red flowers appearing in spring. They feed voraciously on pollen, and their hairy bodies accidentally transport pollen from flower to flower.

Everywhere, beetle specialists are to be found. A small garden in temperate countries may be home to nearly 300 beetle species, and more than 100 of them may live in the compost heap. Each has its own ecological role. Some scavenge on decaying material, several prey on the eggs and larvae of other insects, and still more eat the spores of fungi. Together, they are a team of decomposers, which, along with bacteria and fungi, break down the garden and kitchen waste in the heap to produce a compost that enriches the soil. This job goes on in all kinds of habitats, not just gardens.

## NUT AND WOOD BORERS
In members of the weevil family of beetles, the jaws are mounted on the end of a snout. Species with a short snout, like the Clover weevil, sit astride a leaf and chew its edges. Many weevils have long snouts and they eat leaves by rasping away at the upper layer of cells.

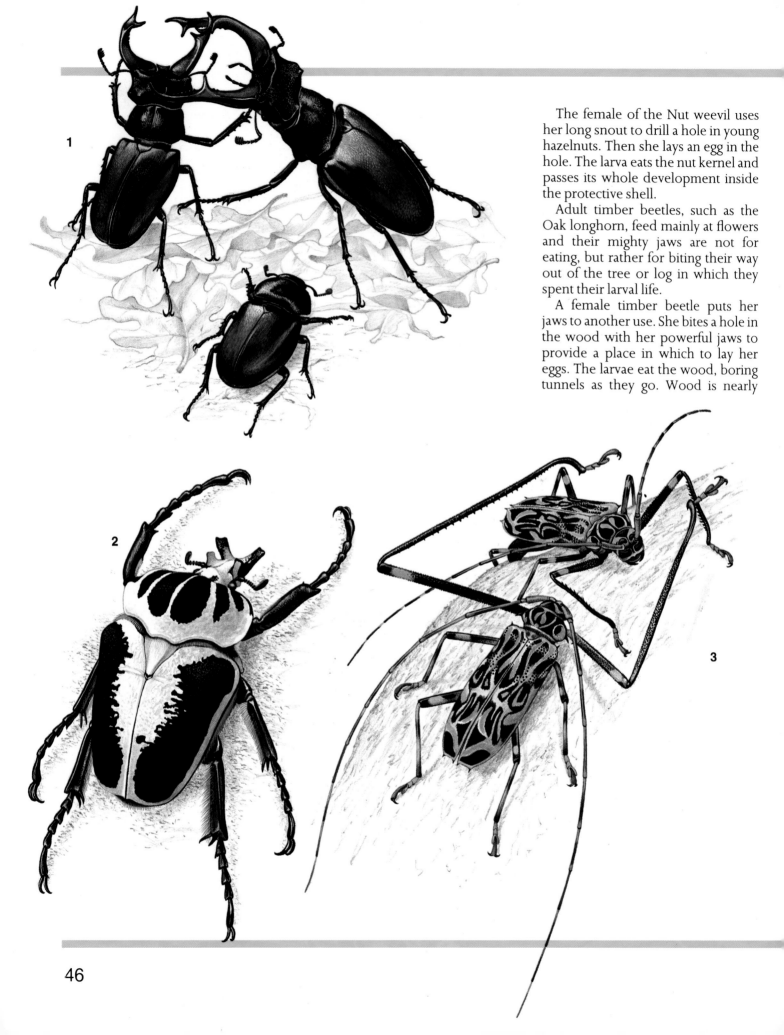

**1**

The female of the Nut weevil uses her long snout to drill a hole in young hazelnuts. Then she lays an egg in the hole. The larva eats the nut kernel and passes its whole development inside the protective shell.

Adult timber beetles, such as the Oak longhorn, feed mainly at flowers and their mighty jaws are not for eating, but rather for biting their way out of the tree or log in which they spent their larval life.

A female timber beetle puts her jaws to another use. She bites a hole in the wood with her powerful jaws to provide a place in which to lay her eggs. The larvae eat the wood, boring tunnels as they go. Wood is nearly

**2**

**3**

indigestible, and the larvae of these beetles, like wood-eating termites, rely on the digestive services of single-celled animals (protozoans) and fungi that live in their guts.

Nevertheless, growth is slow, and some large species of timber beetle may spend several years as larvae.

◀▼A variety of beetles Male Stag beetles (1) in combat over a female. An African Goliath beetle (*Goliathus druryi*) (2). A male Harlequin beetle (*Acrocinus longimanus*) (3) guards his mate as she lays eggs. A male Horned chafer (*Polyphemus* species) (4) feeds on sap. Rival male Rhinoceros beetles (*Dynastes hercules*) (5). A female dung beetle (*Geotrupes* species) (6) and her nest.

There are stories of new adult timber beetles emerging from cricket bats or from the roofing timbers of houses, many years after their wooden homes ceased to be trees.

## COURTSHIP AND MATING

Like all animals, beetles must ensure that their chosen mates are the same species as themselves. This means that before mating, specific recognition signals must be given and received. The signals may involve sight, sound, scent or a combination of all three.

Fireflies can make light-producing chemicals in the tip of the abdomen that are clearly visible at night. The males fly around, switching the glow on and off in a pattern that is unique to the species. The wingless females signal a reply when they recognize the appropriate flashing pattern. Then the males drop down to the females and the beetles mate.

The females of predatory fireflies mimic the light signals of other fireflies, attract the males, and make a meal of them.

Many beetles manufacture special scents called pheromones, that attract mates. Female chafers produce an attractive scent that draws in males from long distances. The males have expanded, comb-like, highly sensitive antennae for receiving these chemical invitations.

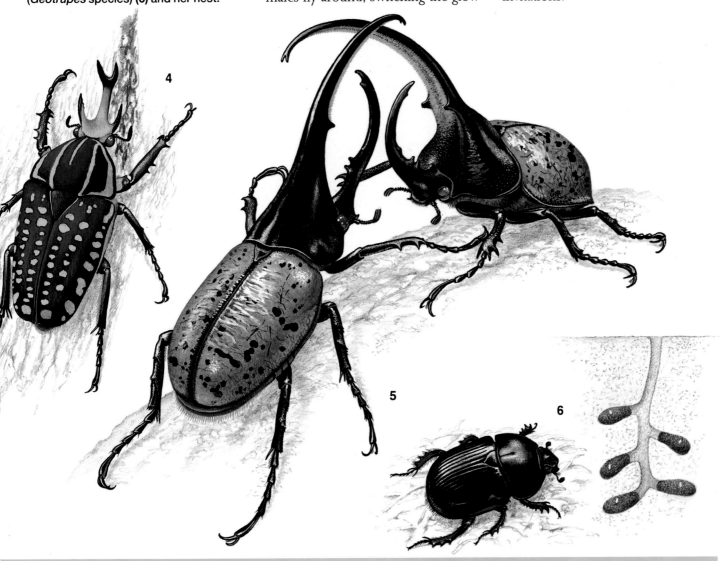

## SIMILAR BUT DIFFERENT

In bark beetles, both the males and females produce a scent that attracts the opposite sex to trees suitable for burrowing and egg-laying. This greatly increases the chances of successful mating. After mating, the females produce another scent, which deters new arrivals, so that the tree does not become overcrowded with beetles. Each male usually remains with his partner, helping her both to make burrows in which she will lay eggs and to guard their offspring.

Both sexes of Deathwatch beetle signal to prospective mates not by scent but by sound. Deep inside old timber, where the beetle develops as a larva, the insects brace their front legs against the tunnels and then tap

▲ In a forest in Trinidad, a female Giant fungus beetle shepherds her larvae to a new fungus, where they will feed. She remains with them until they have molted several times.

rapidly on the tunnel floors with the top of their heads. The signaling season is in spring. People most often hear Deathwatch beetles at night, in old buildings with oak beams. The beetle gets its name from the fact that people sitting up through the night with a dying person were most likely to hear the beetles calling.

In many beetle species, the males and females have a different appearance. This is called sexual dimorphism. Often, as in the Stag beetle, the male has massively developed jaws,

while the female has normally sized ones. Many large tropical beetles, especially in the chafer family, have males with well-developed horns. Usually, these male structures are used as weapons by rival males fighting over a female.

## MATERNAL CARE

The females of some beetles care for their eggs or larvae. Sometimes, as in the tortoise beetles, this is simply a matter of guarding the eggs and young larvae against ants or parasitic wasps. The Giant fungus beetle of South America takes this one stage further. The female stays with her larvae through several molts, shepherding them from one fungus to another.

Burying beetles, like some dung beetles, actually dig a nest in the ground in which to rear their young. The beetles get their name because they bury the bodies of small animals, such as birds or mice. Usually a male and female cooperate in this. The female bites off pieces of flesh from the body and makes them into little balls. She lays eggs in each ball.

The male eventually leaves the nest, but the female remains until after the eggs have hatched. She keeps them clean and feeds them with partially digested meat which she regurgitates for them.

## SELF-DEFENSE

Beetles have many enemies. Other insects, such as dragonflies, assassin bugs and robberflies, prey on them. Insect-eating lizards and birds attack them, as do many mammals.

Beetles, though, have many ways of protecting themselves. Some species make themselves almost invisible by adopting positions where they blend in with their background. In New Guinea, there are weevil species that actually have some mosses and lichen growing on their backs.

Many beetles use chemical warfare against their enemies. Some, like the oil beetles, contain bitter poisons in their elytra, which are brightly colored. Birds learn to associate this warning coloration with a nasty taste and avoid the insects. Both larvae and adults of the familiar ladybirds, such as the Seven-spot, release foul-tasting, bright orange blood when prodded by a predator.

Bombardier beetles produce two chemicals in separate glands at the tip of the abdomen. When disturbed, they squirt a jet of both chemicals at their enemies. When the chemicals mix in the air, there is a short explosion and the predators are covered with a vile, hot and skin-blistering mixture.

►A female of a Viviparous leaf beetle of Brazil lays larvae rather than eggs. As the larvae grow they cover themselves with a protective layer of plant hairs.

▼This Bark timber beetle from Peru is well protected by its resemblance to lichen-covered bark.

# SCORPION FLIES

A female spider has caught a fat, juicy fly in her web. She spins a silken shroud around her booty for safekeeping. She will return for a meal later. But this is one fly she will not eat, for then a scorpion fly lands on her web. Somehow, in a way that no one understands, the scorpion fly walks across the web without becoming entangled or attracting the spider's attention. It deftly removes the spider's trussed-up prey and flies away with it, to make a meal of it for itself.

Scorpion flies are so called because the males of some species have an upturned and swollen tip to the abdomen, which they hold erect similar to a scorpion's tail. Unlike the scorpion, though, there is no sting in the tail. Instead, the swollen tip comprises the male's genital parts.

Scorpion flies are slender insects, with long legs and two pairs of long wings. The head projects into a thick beak-like rostrum that hangs at right angles to the body. The tip of the rostrum bears a pair of biting jaws. There are two long, thread-like antennae, with 16 to 50 segments according to species. The wings have many cross-veins and may be clear and transparent, although in many species they have dark spots or bands.

## INSECT SCAVENGERS

Cool, damp places with lush vegetation are the favorite habitats of most scorpion flies. There, they scavenge on dead plant material, dead insects and even the corpses of small mammals. Some species prey on live insects on the wing, mainly aphids and small flies.

The so-called hanging scorpion flies catch prey in a most unusual way. They hang from a leaf by their forelegs and with their dangling hind legs catch insects as they fly past.

The Common European scorpion fly not only steals prey from the webs of spiders, but often also feeds on pollen and nectar, especially on the flowers of bramble.

In Europe and North America there are several wingless species of scorpion fly that live on high mountains. These have lost the scavenging way of life and instead they feed on mosses. They are called snow scorpion flies because in winter they are often found on snow fields.

## THE FIRST PUPAE

The oldest fossil scorpion flies date from the Permian period (280-225 million years ago), and some species

▲A male Common European scorpion fly eats a dead damselfly. It could not have caught and killed an insect of this size for itself, so it relies on finding dead ones.

found today have hardly changed since the Jurassic period (190-136 million years ago).

Scorpion flies were possibly the first insects to have a complete metamorphosis, with a pupal stage between the larval and adult stages. Although, by insect standards, there are not many living species of scorpion fly, they are an important group. Their ancestors almost certainly gave rise to the true flies, fleas, caddisflies, as well as to the butterflies and moths.

A female scorpion fly lays her eggs in batches on the ground or in soil crevices. In the Common European scorpion fly, eggs hatch after a week and the larvae, which look like caterpillars, feed on rotting plant material or dead insects. They may drag large food items into a short burrow in the soil. The larvae molt their skin seven times before pupating in the soil. The pupae chew a way out of their protective cocoons using their sharp horny jaws (mandibles).

---

## SCORPION FLIES Order
Mecoptera (*less than 400 species*)

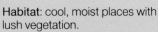 Habitat: cool, moist places with lush vegetation.

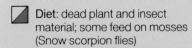 Diet: dead plant and insect material; some feed on mosses (Snow scorpion flies)

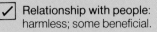 Relationship with people: harmless; some beneficial.

Distribution: worldwide.

Size: length ½-1in.

Color: varied, but many green and yellow patterned with black, or reddish-brown and black.

Species mentioned in text:
Common European scorpion fly
 (*Panorpa communis*)
Hanging scorpion flies (*Bittacus* and
 *Harpobittacus* species)
Snow scorpion flies (*Boreus*
 species)

## ATTRACTED BY SCENT

Scorpion flies are unusual among insects in that it is the male rather than the female that sets out to attract a mate. Males of the Common European scorpion fly, for example, emit a scent from a gland in the abdomen. This attracts females, and when one arrives, the male deposits some saliva on the leaf on which he sits. While the female eats this, he mates with her.

Sometimes, a male will find and guard a dead insect before going through this ritual. This means that he can reward his mate with food as well as a drop of saliva.

## NUPTIAL GIFTS

The males of hanging scorpion flies take this one stage further and offer insect prey to their mates as "wedding" (nuptial) gifts. A male will catch an insect, such as a fly, and then hang from a leaf by his front legs. He transfers the insect from his dangling hind legs to his jaws. At the same time, he emits a musty scent that eventually attracts a female. The male grabs her with his hind legs and there follows a struggle in which he engages his genitals with hers. Once they are joined together by the genitals, he releases the female from the grasp of his hind legs. Now he uses these legs to transfer the prey to within reach of the female's jaws. She grabs it with her legs and begins to feed, while mating continues.

After mating, the male keeps the remains of his gift and may feed on it himself. He may also use it again with other mates, especially since several females may be attracted at the same time to a male with a good juicy gift.

Because female hanging scorpion flies rarely feed, the nuptial gift enables them to produce mature eggs.

◄A mating pair of hanging scorpion flies in Australia. The female is eating a fly presented to her as a nuptial gift by the attendant male.

# FLEAS

A cat returns home and treads warily as soon as she enters the living room. She leaps on to the nearest chair and thereafter prefers to travel round the room by way of the furniture rather than the floor. Her owner is puzzled by this, but the cat knows perfectly well what she is doing. There are newly hatched and hungry Cat fleas in the carpet, and they can jump as high as 13in off the ground. The cat doesn't want another flea infestation.

**FLEAS** Order Siphonaptera
(*about 1,800 species*)

| | Habitat: fur of mammals, feathers of birds. |
|---|---|

Diet: blood; larvae may also eat skin and other debris in nest of host.

Relationship with people: harmful; can transmit disease such as plague.

Distribution: worldwide, as parasites.

Size: length 1/25-1/3in.

Color: yellowish- or reddish-brown to black.

Species mentioned in text:
Arctic hare flea (*Euhoplopsyllus glacialis*)
Cat flea (*Ctenocephalides felis*)
Dog flea (*Ctenocephalus canis*)
European rat flea (*Nosopsyllus fasciatus*)
Human flea (*Pulex irritans*)
Oriental rat flea (*Xenopsylla cheopsis*)
Rabbit flea (*Spilopsyllus cuniculi*)
Tasmanian devil flea (*Uropsylla tasmanica*)

A flea's ability to jump is well known and it is a vital part of its survival kit. Fleas are parasites and live on the bodies of warm-blooded hosts, either birds or mammals. They use their jumping skills to move from host to host, or to get on to a host from their nest material. All species are wingless.

## BRISTLES AND SPINES
A flea is superbly adapted for life as an external parasite. Its body is both flattened from the sides, so that it is much taller than wide, and covered with backward-pointing bristles. This makes it easy for the flea to move forward through an animal's fur or plumage, but not backwards. In fact, a flea seems to "swim" between the hairs or feathers of its host.

In addition to the bristles all over its body, a flea has two sets of spines that form combs, or ctenidia. One set is on the head and protects the eyes. The other set is on the pronotum, a thick plate of exoskeleton at the front of the thorax, and protects the delicate joint between pronotum and mesonotum. Bristles and combs also help to anchor the flea firmly in its host's coat.

Fleas feed entirely on blood. They use their piercing and sucking mouthparts to puncture a small blood vessel just beneath the host's skin. Before sucking the blood, a flea injects a special fluid into the wound that prevents the host's blood from clotting. The process is painless unless the flea touches a skin nerve ending.

About 90 percent of flea species live on mammals, the rest on birds. Each species of flea usually has a special host. Thus, the Cat flea will feed on people, but much prefers the blood of cats. Only aquatic mammals, like whales and seals, and a few land mammals are without fleas.

## A VERY SPECIAL RELATIONSHIP
In the Rabbit flea, the relationship with the host is especially close. The female flea has lost her own sex hormones, and her breeding cycle depends on reproductive hormones in the blood of female rabbits. Thus, a female flea must be on a female rabbit if she is to breed. The flea larvae feed

▼ A Rabbit flea feeds through the soft skin of a rabbit's ear.

on adult fleas' blood droppings, thus forming a further close link between parasite and host.

The Human flea is rare in developed countries and is found mostly on pigs. In evolutionary terms, it probably only recently transferred from pigs to people as hosts when humans began to live a settled existence in caves and shelters. Indeed, it is important for most fleas that their hosts live in groups, whether in dens, nests or houses.

Those species that are found in fur, like the Cat and Dog fleas, lay eggs that drop into the lair or nest material. There, the legless larvae feed on the adult fleas' droppings and on similar debris in the nest. The larvae of the European rat flea beg for food by grabbing an adult at its rear end. This makes the adult flea release blood from its anus. After three molts, the larva pupates in the nest debris.

The larvae of fleas associated with herd animals, such as goats, yaks and horses, live freely and are scattered far and wide, wherever the hosts wander. A few species have larvae, which, like the adults, are parasites on the host. Those of the Arctic hare flea live with the adults in the fur, while larvae of the Tasmanian devil flea burrow into and develop in the skin of the host.

## DISEASE CARRIERS

The Oriental rat flea is responsible for the spread of plague. This deadly bacterial disease is mainly confined to rodents, but fleas biting a person after feeding on an infected rat pass on the germs.

When a rat flea feeds on a host infected with plague, the bacteria stick to spines in a special chamber near the entrance to the flea's stomach. The bacteria multiply and eventually block the gut completely. The hungry flea leaps to another host and bites again and again, but none of the blood can pass the blockage. Instead, it shoots back into the host, carrying with it some of the plague bacteria. In this way a new host becomes infected with plague.

In the great plague outbreak of the 14th century, millions of people died – up to as much as 50 percent of the population in the larger cities of Italy. Plague is still wih us and occasionally breaks out in human populations in North America, the Soviet Union and South-east Asia. This happens when waste disposal services break down and garbage is left close to houses. Flea-infested rats may invade the town and live among the refuse. Sooner or later, they come into contact with people or their pets and, eventually, plague enters the human population.

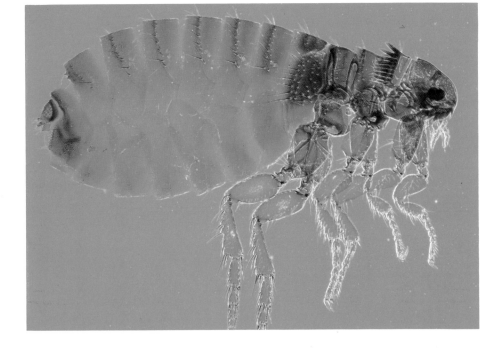

◀A female Dog flea, hugely magnified. The comb of ctenidial spines protects the neck joint.

    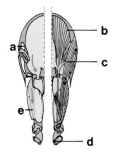

▲A flea can jump with a force 200 times that of gravity. No muscle could do this; fleas use the energy stored in a special structure (a) made of a highly elastic protein called resilin.

Muscles (b) and (c) compress this structure, while special plates lock the three segments of the thorax. The flea rests on the trochanters (d). When stimulated to jump, the flea relaxes the muscles and the energy stored in the resilin is conducted down the ridge (e), causing the recoil that launches the flea.

# FLIES

The hedgerow abounds with insects. Above, male hoverflies guard aerial territories. Below, brightly colored flies, feed at hawthorn blossoms for pollen and nectar. In the hedge bottom shade, a flesh fly lays eggs in the nostrils of a dead mouse. And, flitting from flower to flower, a robberfly preys on other insects.

## FLIES Order Diptera
*(at least 90,000 species)*

 **Habitat**: all possible habitats.

 **Diet**: all kinds of liquid food.

 **Relationship with people**: many beneficial as scavengers, killers of insect pests; others pests of crops or carriers of disease.

**Distribution**: worldwide.

**Size**: length 1/50–2in.

**Color**: many dull drab, others brightly marked with various patterns.

**Species mentioned in text:**
Beech gall midge (*Mikiola fagi*)
Bluebottle (blowfly) (*Calliphora vomitoria*)
California seaweed fly (*Ephydra californica*)
Cranefly (*Tipula lunata*)
Housefly (*Musca domestica*)
Knapweed gallfly (*Urophora jaceana*)
Malaria mosquito (*Anopheles gambiae*)
Petrol fly (*Heleomyia petrolei*)
Red-footed robberfly (*Cyrtopogon rufipes*)
Scalar scuttle-fly (*Megaselia scalaris*)
Tsetse flies (*Glossina* species)
Tumbu fly (*Cordylobia anthropophaga*)
Yellow dung fly (*Scathophaga stercoraria*)

This impressive range of life-styles can be seen among flies in just a short stretch of hedgerow anywhere in northern Europe or North America. On a worldwide basis, the variety of flies is truly amazing. These insects have invaded nearly all habitats in most parts of the world.

All true flies share one unique and important feature: they have only one pair of working wings, the front pair. This gives flies great speed and agility in flight. Many flies can hover and fly backwards, and some midges can beat their wings 1,000 times per second!

## MASTERS OF FLIGHT

Much of a fly's abilities in the air is possible because of what has happened during evolution to the hind wings. They have not been lost, but instead have become highly modified structures called halteres. Each haltere is shaped like a drumstick, with a round head at the tip of a thin stalk. Special sense organs at the base of each haltere tell the fly how fast it is flying, the angle and speed of turns and changes in direction it makes, and if it is being blown off course.

The aerial acrobatics of flies relies also on good eyesight, and flies have large eyes with acute vision. Many species are sensitive to the slightest movement, as anyone who has tried to catch a hoverfly knows very well. Claws and special pads on the feet, coupled with excellent sight and mastery of the air, allow flies to perform seemingly impossible feats such as landing upside down on ceilings!

## LIQUID FEEDERS

All flies have sucking mouthparts. They have one or, in some cases, two powerful muscular pumps within the large and mobile head. This enables flies to cope with a wide range of liquid foods. Many lap up nectar at flowers and the honeydew produced by aphids. Others feed on the fluids associated with rotting plants or dead animals.

▼Three flies to avoid: the Tumbu fly (1) of Africa, whose larva (1a) burrows under the skin of people. A bloodsucking tsetse (2), whose bite can pass on the blood parasite causing sleeping sickness. The Malaria mosquito (3) passes on the parasite causing malaria.

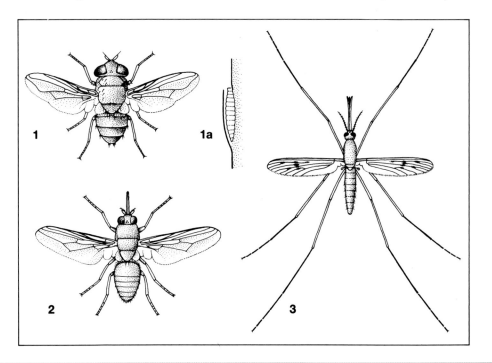

Robberflies have added a piercing ability to their sucking mouthparts and feed on the body fluids of other insects. Some, like the mosquitoes and gnats, specialize in piercing the skin of reptiles, birds and mammals and sucking their blood.

## WASP AND BEE MIMICS

Many flower-visiting flies are brightly colored. With patterns of black and yellow or black and orange bands, several species are more than passable imitations (mimics) of wasps. Others are furry and closely resemble bees in color pattern.

Almost all of these effective mimics of wasps and bees are fast-flying hoverflies. Their close resemblance to stinging insects is no accident. When a young and inexperienced insect-feeding bird pecks at a wasp or bee, it is likely to suffer a painful sting. The bird associates this distressing experience with the bright colors of these insects and remembers to avoid them. When the bird sees other wasp- or bee-mimicking hoverflies, it mistakes them for insects with a sting in their tails and leaves them well alone.

## LOVE SIGNALS...

Many flies have very interesting and strange courtship rituals. Males of the Knapweed gallfly signal to females by waving their patterned wings in a kind of semaphore.

A male of the Red-footed robberfly from Europe stands in front of his intended mate and raises the shiny black tip of his abdomen into the air; he bobs it up and down while weaving from side to side. He edges nearer and begins to stroke her head with his front feet. If the female is receptive, he mounts her from behind and mates with her.

Males of the Yellow dungfly seek females at fresh dung, where mating takes place. After mating, the male remains on top of his mate while she lays eggs. This prevents other males from mating with her. By guarding her in this way, the male ensures that his sperm fertilizes the eggs and he is the father of the offspring.

## ...AND LOVE GIFTS

The strangest mating rituals are found among the dance, or assassin, flies. These flies prey on other insects and suck their body fluids. The males also catch small insects, which they offer to

▼Unusual species of fly: Two male stalk-eyed flies, *Diopsis* species **(1)**, from Africa, use their eye-stalks as yardsticks to assess each other's size in a contest over territory. The winner mates with any females that enter the territory. The eyes of the females are not stalked. This beautiful South American robberfly, *Mallophora fascipennis* **(2)**, is a superb mimic of a female orchid bee *Eulaema fasciata* (above), on which it preys.

females as a kind of "love gift." The male hangs from the edge of a leaf by his front legs, supporting both himself and a female. While they mate, the female eats the offering.

The males of some dance flies wrap their gift in white silk, which makes it easier for females to see it. The males of some species cheat by offering a very small gift wrapped in a very large silk package. Yet other species take the deception even further and offer an empty package. In many species, the male takes the gift away from the female after mating and uses it again with another mate.

## LARVAL LIFE

The larvae of flies are blind, legless and usually creamy white. Almost all develop and feed in moist or damp places. The females, therefore, take great care in laying their eggs in just the right places. Thus, females of the Yellow dungfly lay their eggs in fresh cow dung. Larvae of the bluebottle (blowfly) develop from eggs laid on dead animals. The larvae feed on the corpse and help dispose of it.

Houseflies spend their larval life in almost any suitable decaying matter. Some species develop as parasites inside the bodies of other insects, especially caterpillars.

## SPECIALISTS AND GENERALISTS

There are flies whose larvae specialize in living in the most unlikely and hostile places. Those of the Petrol fly live in natural seepages of crude oil, where they feed on trapped insects. Several related species live in hot-water springs, while larvae of the Californian seaweed fly live in salt water, often in such large numbers that North American and Mexican

Indians used them as food. One family of flies has larvae which eat almost nothing but slugs and snails.

If specialization is a major feature of fly larvae, there are also some species that are not so choosy. Thus, the larvae of the Scalar scuttle-fly are known to have fed quite happily on emulsion paint, shoe polish, dead bodies pickled in formalin and the lungs of living people!

After molting its skin several times, a fly larva then pupates. In the more advanced flies, pupation takes place within the last larval skin. This is a darkened, specially hardened casing called the puparium.

▲ A larva of the Beech gall midge has induced a beech leaf to develop these galls, on which it then feeds.

▶ A male cranefly. His halteres, or modified hind wings appear as a pair of drumsticks behind the forewings.

▶ A female Malaria mosquito sucks blood from a person. Millions of people in the tropics die each year from malaria, which is passed on by mosquitoes.

# CADDIS FLIES

The muddy bottom of a pond is still and quiet. It is littered with dead leaves and sticks. Suddenly, one of the sticks· begins to move. Slow and lumbering, it wanders to the stem of a water weed and begins to climb. The stick appears to have a head, which begins to feed on the weed. It is not a stick at all, but a northern caddis larva, protected by a case of tiny twiglets.

## CADDIS FLIES Order Trichoptera (*about 5,000 species*)

 **Habitat:** cool, damp areas; larvae aquatic, some in sea water.

 **Diet:** adults rarely feed; larvae eat algae, plant tissue, small water creatures.

**Relationship with people:** beneficial as important food in freshwater fisheries, but larvae of some species are pests of rice paddies.

**Distribution:** worldwide.

**Size:** length ½-1½in.

**Color:** drab; usually brown or gray-brown.

**Species mentioned in text:**
Marine caddis fly (*Philanisus plebeius*)
Northern caddis flies (*Limnephilus* species)
Snail-case caddis flies (*Helicopsyche* species)
White caddis fly (*Hectopsyche albida*)

Many people know caddis flies best as larvae. Anyone who has been pond-dipping with a net will have seen the beautifully made cases that the larvae build around themselves for protection. As for the adults, most people would pass them off as rather drab moths, with long antennae. When at rest, the adults resemble moths in that they hold the wings roof-like over the abdomen.

## TINY HAIRS AND JAWS
As adults, caddis flies differ from the moths in several ways. First, their wings are not covered with tiny overlapping scales but are clothed with tiny hairs. Second, while the mouth-parts of caddis flies are used to suck up liquid food, they are reduced in size and are not modified into a long, tubular proboscis. There are two sets of palps and the minutest traces of jaws. Although some species feed on nectar at flowers, numerous others probably never feed at all.

A third difference is that most caddis flies are poor fliers, with a slow, fluttering flight. A few strong-flying species join together their front and hind wings in flight by means of long curved hairs.

Caddis flies are mainly active at dusk and at night. They rarely stray far from streams, ponds and lakes. During the day, they rest in cool, dark places.

mating takes place on the wing. In a number of other species, both sexes "dance" in large swarms over water. The females search for and recognize males by their flight movements.

Female caddis flies lay eggs in slimy masses or in string-like threads. They deposit these on stones or plant stems close to or in the water. The females of some species actually climb down into the water to attach their eggs to submerged stones.

Caddis flies are often choosy about the type of water they frequent. Some species like small, still, muddy ponds. Others favor very fast-flowing streams with gravel bottoms. A few live in rivers, while larvae of the Marine caddis fly of southern Australia and New Zealand grow and develop in rock pools by the sea.

## UNDERWATER HOUSES

The larvae of caddis flies are caterpillar-like, and in most species they feed on plants and various small water animals. They breathe by means of long, abdominal, thread-like gills.

In general, the larvae build for themselves protective cases in which they live and grow. The building materials used include sand grains, snail shells, stones and small lengths of stem. The case is held together by silk or glue made by the larvae. Most cases are straight or slightly curved, although snail-case caddis flies build a coiled case like a snail's shell. Some of these larvae prey on small water creatures, which they grab with their front legs and pull back to the case.

A few larvae do not build cases, but instead spin a silk web between underwater stems or stones. The web faces upstream and catches mainly water fleas, on which the larvae feed.

Caddis fly larvae are an important food for some fish and the larvae of other insects. They do not tolerate pollution and their presence (or absence) is a good indicator of the cleanliness of the water.

▲A northern caddis fly pupa wriggles away from its case on its way to emerging from the water as an adult.

◄A caddis fly egg mass on a rush. On hatching, the larvae drop to the pond below and develop in the water.

## MATING SWARMS

Caddis flies mate only once a year. They spend the winter as larvae, and pupate in the spring. Adults emerge in summer and immediately set up mating swarms.

In some species, such as the White caddis fly of North America, females swarm in large numbers over water, usually near a prominent clump of rushes. This attracts the males, and

# MOTHS

In an East African savannah, vultures have picked clean the bones of a dead elephant. But there is still something edible left: the skin of the elephant's feet. This is covered with a dense web of silk, and inside, many caterpillars feed on this unlikely food. Eventually, they will become moths and fly off in search of a different type of animal remains.

This may seem a very unusual way of life for a moth. But in wardrobes all over the world, close relatives of these African skin-feeders are munching away on woollen sweaters. They are the caterpillars of clothes moths, and the wool they eat is made of the same material as skin. Moths are so successful because their larvae have adapted to a wide range of foods.

Most people think of moths as drab, night-flying relatives of the butterflies, with antennae lacking a club tip. In fact, there are many day-flying moths, with clubbed antennae and bright colors. The distinction between moths and butterflies is really only a matter of convenience; it does not reflect real relationships. Indeed, there are some groups of moth that are more closely related to butterflies than they are to other moths.

▼A South African emperor moth lays her eggs. Female moths identify their larval food plants by sight and smell.

**MOTHS** Order Lepidoptera
(*at least 181,000 species*)

 Habitat: wherever there are plants.

 Diet: larvae mainly eat plants; adults nectar-feeders, some suck blood of mammals.

 Relationship with people: many pests of crops, a few beneficial as pollinators.

Distribution: almost worldwide.

Size: wingspan 1/8-12in.

Color: many drab, others vividly and warningly colored.

Species mentioned in text:
Bloodsucking moth (*Calpe eustrigata*)
Cinnabar moth (*Tyria jacobaeae*)
Death's-head hawkmoth (*Acherontia atropos*)
East African uraniid moth (*Chrysiridia croesus*)
Emperor gum moth (*Antheraea eucalypti*)
Garden tiger moth (*Arctia caja*)
Oriental fruit moth (*Grapholitha molesta*)
Oriental tear moth (*Lobocraspis griseifusa*)
Puss moth (*Cerura vinula*)
Red-underwing moth (*Catocala nupta*)
South African emperor moth (*Gonimbrasia belina*)
Zodiac moth (*Alcides zodiaca*)

▲ This day-flying moth from New Guinea and Australia spends its days feeding at flowers near the ground.

◄ A caterpillar of the Death's-head hawkmoth feeds on a poisonous plant of the potato family. The adults often migrate north to Europe from Africa.

## SCALY WINGS, LONG PROBOSCIS

The wings of moths are covered with dense overlapping scales, rather like the tiles on a roof. The scales make up the "dust" that gets rubbed off if the insects are handled.

The color patterns of their wings, whether drab or colorful, are due to the scales. Beneath the scales are glassy membranes, stiffened by veins.

Moths have long tubular sucking mouthparts. The tongue, or proboscis, is coiled up under the head when not in use. Adult moths feed mainly on nectar, although the Oriental tear moth clusters around the eyes of buffalo and cattle and drinks their tears. The Bloodsucker moth, also from the Far East, goes even further. It uses its proboscis to pierce the skin of mammals and sucks their blood.

Some primitive moths have no proboscis but only jaws, which they use to grind up pollen grains.

## A WORLD OF SCENT

Because most moths fly at night, the males and females use scents known as pheromones to find each other.

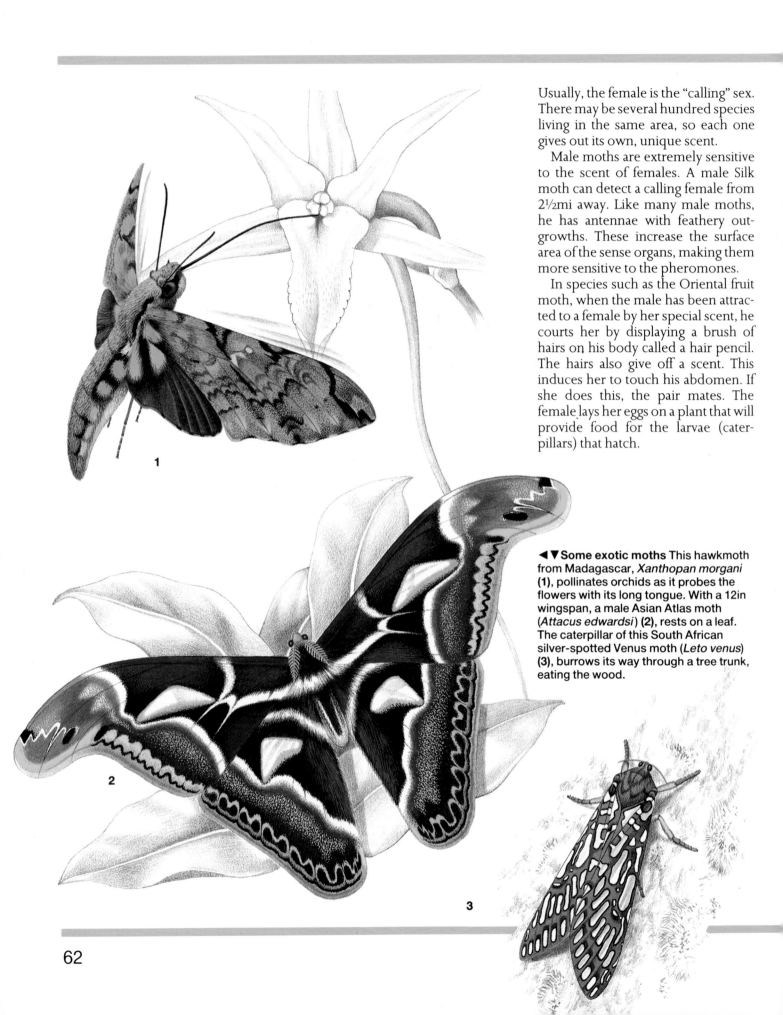

Usually, the female is the "calling" sex. There may be several hundred species living in the same area, so each one gives out its own, unique scent.

Male moths are extremely sensitive to the scent of females. A male Silk moth can detect a calling female from 2½mi away. Like many male moths, he has antennae with feathery outgrowths. These increase the surface area of the sense organs, making them more sensitive to the pheromones.

In species such as the Oriental fruit moth, when the male has been attracted to a female by her special scent, he courts her by displaying a brush of hairs on his body called a hair pencil. The hairs also give off a scent. This induces her to touch his abdomen. If she does this, the pair mates. The female lays her eggs on a plant that will provide food for the larvae (caterpillars) that hatch.

◀▼Some exotic moths This hawkmoth from Madagascar, *Xanthopan morgani* (1), pollinates orchids as it probes the flowers with its long tongue. With a 12in wingspan, a male Asian Atlas moth (*Attacus edwardsi*) (2), rests on a leaf. The caterpillar of this South African silver-spotted Venus moth (*Leto venus*) (3), burrows its way through a tree trunk, eating the wood.

## DEFENSE IN A HOSTILE WORLD

From the moment each moth caterpillar hatches, it is surrounded by enemies. Parasitic wasps want to lay their eggs in it. Birds with hungry chicks to feed seek out the caterpillar.

The caterpillar may be a slow-moving eating machine, but it is not defenseless. Many moth caterpillars match the green color of the leaves on which they feed. This camouflage is usually effective against birds, but not against parasitic wasps, which detect their prey by scent and touch.

One way of getting around this is to be hairy, like the "woolly bear" caterpillars of the Garden tiger moth. The hairs make it difficult for the wasp to walk over the caterpillar's body. They also make for a nasty beakful if a bird should try and eat it. Some caterpillars, like those of the Emperor gum moth of Australia, are covered in poisonous spines, which snap off in the skin of a predator, causing pain.

The European Puss moth caterpillar has a battery of defenses at its disposal. It can rear up both ends of its body in a threat display. It deters parasitic wasps by waving a pair of filaments at the rear of its body. If these are not enough, it can squirt out a jet of formic acid.

Chemical defense is used by many moth caterpillars. The vivid black and yellow colors of the Cinnabar caterpillar is a clear warning to birds to keep away. The larvae are poisonous because they absorb poisons from their food plants, groundsel and ragwort. The plants evolved the poisons to deter grazing mammals, but the Cinnabar caterpillars in time became immune to them.

## FRIGHTENING BEHAVIOR

After molting its skin several times, the moth caterpillar spins a silk cocoon, within which it pupates. The tough silk is itself a defense for the otherwise helpless pupa, or chrysalis.

Adult moths are also surrounded by enemies, mainly insect-eating birds. They, too, have a range of defense mechanisms. The night-flying moths roost by day, with their wings angled over their abdomen, and they are usually well camouflaged. In the Red underwing, the wing pattern resembles lichen-covered bark. If disturbed, this moth suddenly exposes its brightly patterned red and black hind wings, which startles the bird.

In similar circumstances, various species of emperor moth expose the conspicuous eyespots on their hind wings. These staring "eyes" frighten the bird away.

Day-flying moths, such as the Cinnabar and burnet species are often warningly colored. They inherit the poisons from their larvae. Some adult tiger moths have two lines of defense. During the day, their warning colors advertise a foul taste to would-be predators. By night, they produce very high-pitched sound waves. These deter bats, which use the echo of their own high-pitched sounds to locate flying insects.

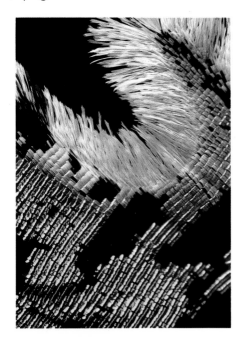

▲ Highly magnified, the shiny wing scales of this tropical uraniid moth glimmer and glint in the sunlight.

◄ In Victorian times, the brilliant, shiny wings of this East African day-flying uraniid moth were made into ladies' jewelry such as brooches.

# BUTTERFLIES

In the dappled sunlight of a woodland glade in spring, a Speckled wood butterfly confronts another and chases it away in an upward, spiraling flight. Afterwards, it returns to its roost on the ground. The butterfly is a male defending his territory, a brightly lit patch in the glade. He drives away other males and mates with any willing females that enter his warm, sunny area.

Although butterflies, with their wide range of size, shape and attractive colors, have always been one of the best known groups of insects, they were mainly studied as interesting museum specimens. Only recently was it discovered that many butterfly species occupy and defend territories. Today we know them as a successful group of insects with a wide range of unusual and interesting behaviors.

Like the moths (see pages 60-63), butterflies have large wings covered with overlapping, microscopic scales. The scales are responsible for the color patterns on the wings.

## STARTING ON THE RIGHT PLANT
Butterflies, like moths, have a larval (caterpillar) stage and a pupal (chrysalis) stage before becoming adult.

► **Look-alike in African butterflies**
Two highly poisonous and distasteful butterflies, the Plain tiger (*Danaus chrysippus*) (1), and the Friar (*Amauris niavius*) (2), are the models for two different female look-alike forms of the Mocker swallowtail (3, 4). The male swallowtail (5) is not a look-alike (mimic).

---

**BUTTERFLIES** Order Lepidoptera (*about 20,000 species*)

 **Habitat:** wherever there are plants.

 **Diet:** caterpillars plant-feeders; adults mainly drink nectar.

☑ **Relationship with people:** a few crop pests, some pollinators; most are beneficial by virtue of the visual pleasure they give.

**Distribution:** almost worldwide, including polar fringes.

**Size:** wingspan 1/3-7 1/2 in.

**Color:** a few drab browns, but mainly brightly patterned with yellow, blues, red, orange, often with eyespots.

**Species mentioned in text:**
African dry-leaf butterfly (*Precis tugela*)
African mocker swallowtail (*Papilio dardanus*)
Antelope butterfly (*Hypolimnas antilope*)

Cabbage white (*Pieris brassicae*)
Comma butterfly (*Polygonia c-album*)
Coolie butterfly (*Anartia amathea*)
Ethil helicon (*Heliconius ethilla*)
Grayling (*Hipparchia semele*)
Green hairstreak (*Callophrys rubi*)
King page swallowtail (*Papilio thoas*)
Malayan dry-leaf butterfly (*Kallima paralekta*)
Monarch butterfly (*Danaus plexippus*)
Painted lady (*Vanessa cardui*)
Passion vine helicon (*Heliconius hecale*)
Speckled wood (*Pararge aegeria*)

2

4

The caterpillars of many butterfly species are specialists and can eat the leaves of only one plant species or a few closely related ones. This means that the female has to be extremely choosy about where she lays her eggs. Females of the Cabbage white butterfly, for example, recognize cabbage plants and their relatives by the smell of mustard oil given off by the leaves.

In many butterflies, the female first searches a leaf for the eggs of other females before laying her own. If there are too many alien eggs she goes elsewhere. By doing this, she avoids condemning her offspring to overcrowding, where food may run out and disease may spread.

This avoidance of all plants that already bear butterfly eggs is exploited by the Blue passion flower of South America. The plant has round, yellow swellings on its leaflets, which look just like the eggs of the Ethil helicon butterfly. This persuades the female helicons to lay eggs elsewhere, although some always do lay eggs on the plant. Thus the plant limits the numbers of eggs that the butterflies lay and therefore restricts the amount of damage to its leaves.

## ON GUARD

For most butterflies, choosing the right foodplant for her offspring is the only parental care given by the female. However, in the Philippines, females of the Antilope butterfly watch over their egg batches until they hatch and the caterpillars move away.

►Only a few minutes old, this fresh pupa of a Comma butterfly will spend the winter in this state.

Butterfly eggs may be spindle- or lens-shaped or simply round. They are often beautifully sculptured, with patterns of ridges or scalloping. The sculpturing is characteristic of the species and is used in identification.

## PREPARING FOR THE CHANGE
The caterpillars eat the remains of their egg shells immediately after hatching. Thereafter, they live up to their reputation as voracious eating machines. They sit astride a stem or straddle the edge of a leaf, using their powerful jaws like a pair of scissors.

Each caterpillar grows rapidly and molts its skin four times before it pupates. Shortly before pupation, it ceases feeding and seeks a suitable place in which to carry out the transformation to a beautiful butterfly. This may be in the ground, under loose bark or out in the open.

Those species that pupate in the soil dig out a small chamber and line it with silk from glands in the head. Others, such as the Comma, suspend themselves upside-down from a twig or branch, attached by a pad of silk. The swallowtails suspend themselves head upwards by a thin girdle of silk around the thorax.

## THE LAST STEP TO ADULTHOOD
Soon after settling, the chrysalis (or pupa) to-be wriggles its way out of the last larval skin and its cuticle hardens and darkens.

The pupa stage may last as little as a week in tropical countries, but it often persists for up to several months in cool, temperate areas, where the insect passes the winter in this stage.

When the adult butterfly is ready to emerge, the pupal skin splits along a line of weakness on the top of the thorax. The new adult hangs from the pupal skin or a stem while it inflates its crumpled wings by pumping blood through their veins, and its cuticle dries and hardens. It then flies off and finds its first meal of nectar at a flower.

## SIGNALS FOR SURVIVAL
The color patterns and shapes of both larval and adult butterflies are signals to the outside world. These signals include both false and true messages. False messages are all designed to fool predators, especially birds. For example, the young larva of the King page swallowtail of South America mimics (resembles) a fresh, shiny bird dropping that has just landed on a leaf. The pupae of species like the Comma butterfly look like crumpled, dead leaves and similarly are overlooked by birds.

Dead-leaf mimics are also found among the adults of many species. The undersides of the wings of both the Malayan and African dry-leaf butterflies are mottled gray-brown, and divided by a dark line resembling the midrib of a leaf. Both have tails on the hind wings that look like leaf stalks. The butterflies rest on vegetation with their wings folded over the body. In this position, they are very difficult to see. But when they take to the wing, there is a sudden splash of color, for the uppersides of the wings are brightly colored. This startles any would-be predator.

## A SICKENING EXPERIENCE
Most of the true messages signaled by caterpillars and adult butterflies are to do with being poisonous or foul-tasting and they involve bright, eye-catching color patterns. Instead of saying "I am not really here," the message from these warningly colored species is: "Look at me and my bright colors and remember them: I taste awful and will make you ill."

▶Males of the South American butterfly *Actinote alcione* feeding on dung fallen among some leaves. They are replacing salts lost during mating, when each deposits a sperm package (spermatophore) in the female.

As with poisonous moths, many butterflies store plant poisons during their caterpillar stage and these persist in the adult. Poisonous species such as the Monarch, one of the milkweed butterflies, have warning coloration, both as adults and as caterpillars. Any bird that is foolish enough to eat them becomes violently sick. It soon learns to associate the insects' colors with the sickness and avoids these butterflies thereafter.

## FOOLING THE MEMORY

Butterflies with warning coloration take advantage of the fact that birds have both good eyesight and a good memory. This is taken further in many tropical areas, where quite unrelated species of poisonous butterflies often have very similar patterns of warning coloration. This is a type of mimicry called Müllerian mimicry, named after the German naturalist Fritz Müller, who first discovered it.

The advantage to the butterflies is that where several different distasteful or poisonous species live in the same area, the local insect-eating birds have to learn to avoid only one kind of color pattern. This means that fewer butterflies are injured or killed while inexperienced birds are still learning which color patterns to avoid. Also, the damage suffered by the butterflies is evenly spread among the species.

## TASTY AND FOUL LOOK-ALIKES

In another kind of mimicry, a species of butterfly that is neither poisonous nor distasteful, has the same warning coloration as another, extremely unpleasant species. This is known as Batesian mimicry, after its discoverer the English naturalist H. W. Bates.

Here, the true poisonous species is called the model. For the system to work properly, the tasty mimic species must never outnumber the models, because an increasing number of birds would otherwise soon learn that the majority of species with warning coloration are quite tasty.

The mimics get around this in a very ingenious way. A local population of butterfles will mimic two or even more species of distasteful models, instead of just one. By doing this, they reduce the number of mimics for each model. The best known example is the African mocker swallowtail, in which only the females are look-alikes. They resemble several different species of milkweed butterfly over their range in Africa. Two of the commonest models are the Plain tiger and the Friar butterflies (see illustration on pages 64-65).

## COURTSHIP AND MATING

Mating in butterflies almost always follows an elaborate courtship ritual staged or started by the male. This may involve the male hovering over the female or both sexes spiraling around each other in flight.

In many species the sexes recognize each other by the characteristic markings on their wings. But because of mimicry, appearances can be deceptive. This is where scent becomes important. In many of the skipper butterflies, for example, the males have scent-producing pouches on the

◀A mating pair of Coolie butterflies in Trinidad. The male (above) and female have different colors. This is known as sexual dimorphism.

forewings. They flutter these in front of a female and if she is receptive, it induces her to mate.

A male of the grayling of Europe makes sure that the female gets the message by clasping his forewings over her antennae. This rubs off some special scent-laden wing scales called androconia. If she is receptive, the male moves to her rear and they mate. There is no doubt that scent is very important for courtship and mating in many, if not all, butterfly species.

## MIGRATING BUTTERFLIES
Many butterflies are powerful fliers and can fly long distances. Species such as the Painted lady regularly migrate. This butterfly lives in most parts of the world. In Mexico it breeds in winter and in some years migrates north through the United States, as far

as Canada. The same species regularly migrates from North Africa into Europe, as far north as Iceland. In the spring of 1988, the clouds of Painted lady butterflies migrating west from the deserts of Iraq and Jordan were dense enough in Israel to slow down traffic on the road running north from the Dead Sea.

The most famous migrant is the Monarch. Each spring, millions of these butterflies migrate north from Mexico into the north-eastern United States. There they pass through several generations during the summer. In the fall, flocks of them fly south to Mexico. It was only in 1976 that their hibernation site was discovered. It is a valley in Michoacan State, at an altitude of 10,000ft. Here as many as 14 million Monarch butterflies cluster on trees in an area of only 3½ acres.

▲ Having uncoiled its long proboscis, this butterfly probes the flowers of lantana for nectar in Costa Rica.

▼ The Green hairstreak butterfly roosts on a leaf, camouflaged by the green undersides of its wings.

# WASPS

**Black and yellow wasps are unwelcome visitors to a garden picnic. They are seeking sugary foods like jam. Nearby other members of the insect raiding party are at work. Some are stripping wood fibers from an old fence post, while others are preying on flies.**

**WASPS** Order Hymenoptera
(*at least 200,000 species*)

**Habitat:** wherever there are plants.

**Diet:** larvae feed on or in host insect or on prey provided by the female; a few eat plant tissue; adults are nectar-feeders.

**Relationship with people:** mainly beneficial as killers of pest insects.

**Distribution:** almost worldwide.

**Size:** length 1/100-2in.

**Color:** varied, from all black to patterns of yellow and/or red and black, metallic green, blue, bronze.

Species mentioned in text:
Alder wood wasp (*Xiphydria camelus*)
Cabbage braconid (*Apanteles glomeratus*)
European pine sawfly (*Neodiprion sertifer*)
Giant wood wasp (*Urocerus gigas*)
Hornet (*Vespa* species)
Ichneumon wasp (e.g., *Pseudorhyssa, Rhysella* species)
Yellow-footed braconid (*Apanteles flavipes*)

These wasps are the "yellow-jackets" familiar to everyone. They are social insects and live in colonies. But the majority of wasps have solitary lifestyles. Most of these species have larvae that all develop as parasites of other insects. The females of some solitary wasps are nest-builders and hunt insect prey as the sole source of food for their larvae.

## SAWFLIES AND WOOD WASPS

The most primitive wasps are the sawflies, so called because the females have an egg-laying tube, or ovipositor, which has serrated blades like a saw. The female uses this to insert eggs into the tissues of plants.

The larvae of most sawflies resemble caterpillars and have a similar way of life to theirs, eating leaves and stems. Many are specialists on one, or a group of closely related, host plants. Some larvae are pests, such as those of the European pine sawfly, which can seriously damage young trees by stripping them of their needles.

Allied to the sawflies are the horntails and wood wasps. Larvae of the Giant wood wasp bore through and eat the solid timber of spruce trunks. They transmit a fungus disease that may eventually kill the trees.

## WINGS AND WAISTLINE

All wasps have two pairs of wings. In sawflies and wood wasps, these have a complex network of veins. When in flight, the wasp's front wings are coupled to the hind wings by a row of little hooks on the leading edge of each hind wing. The hooks latch on to a fold on the rear edge of the forewing.

In primitive wasps, the abdomen is broadly attached to the thorax. In all other species there is a narrow "wasp waist" between the thorax and abdomen. The waist is the result of a narrowing between the first and the second abdominal segments.

## PARASITIC WASPS

Almost all kinds of insect are attacked by parasitic wasps. There are even tiny wasps called chalcids that lay their eggs in the eggs of other insects. Some chalcids lay their eggs in the larvae of other parasitic wasps.

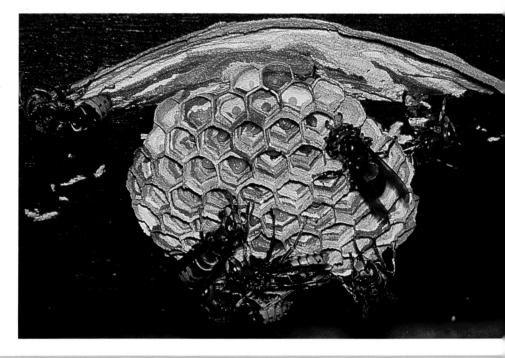

▼Workers of a European hornet tend larvae in their six-sided cells. The paper nest is made from chewed wood fibers.

▲ More than 50 parasitic braconid wasp larvae have fed inside this dying caterpillar and have burst out to spin cocoons and pupate.

◄ A female ichneumon wasp drills with her ovipositor to lay an egg in a hidden Alder wood wasp larva. The wasp behind – a different species – will lay her egg in the same hole and her larva will eat those of the ichneumon and wood wasps.

## A SLOW DEATH FOR THE HOST

Many parasitic wasps attack only one species of insect. Others lay their eggs in any exposed insect larva or pupa.

Female parasitic wasps often have long ovipositors for laying their eggs in host larvae hidden deep in wood. Many deposit the eggs in or on the caterpillars of butterflies and moths. Each wasp larva eats the insides of the host, which eventually dies. After several molts, the larva spins a cocoon inside the host's body or on its surface before changing to an adult.

Because many parasitic wasps attack only one host, some have been used as natural control agents for pests. In Barbados, the Yellow braconid wasp is used to keep down the numbers of the Sugarcane stem borer, a moth caterpillar. Farmers and gardeners in Europe and North America have an ally in the Cabbage apanteles, a wasp whose larvae kill caterpillars of the Cabbage white butterfly.

## HUNTING SPECIES

Hunting wasps differ from parasitic wasps in two important ways. First, they do not use the ovipositor as an egg-laying tube. Instead, it has become a sting for injecting poison into insect prey. Second, they provide a safe place, the nest, in which the prey is stored for their larvae to feed on.

Having a nest requires that the wasp can find its way home after a hunting trip. Wasps (and bees) do this by memorizing both near and distant landmarks around the nest on special "orientation flights" just after the nest is completed. They also use the position of the Sun in the sky as an additional guide.

According to species, the nest may be a simple or branching burrow in the ground or soft, dead wood. Some hunting wasps use the old burrows of wood-boring beetles. A few collect mud, which they use to build exposed nests on stones.

Whatever the nest type, each contains a number of special chambers called cells. A single larva develops in each one, feeding on stung and paralyzed insects caught by the mother wasp. Each wasp species specializes on a particular kind of prey, such as caterpillars, flies, beetles or spiders.

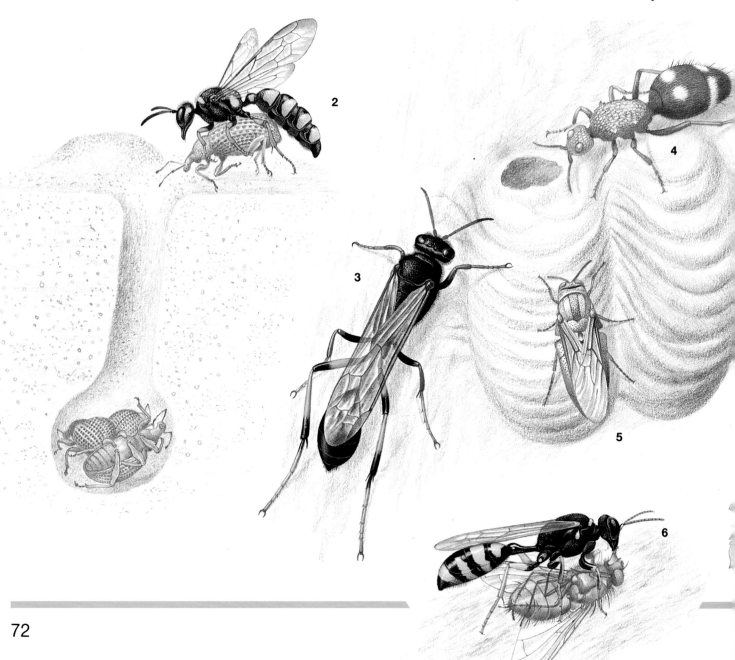

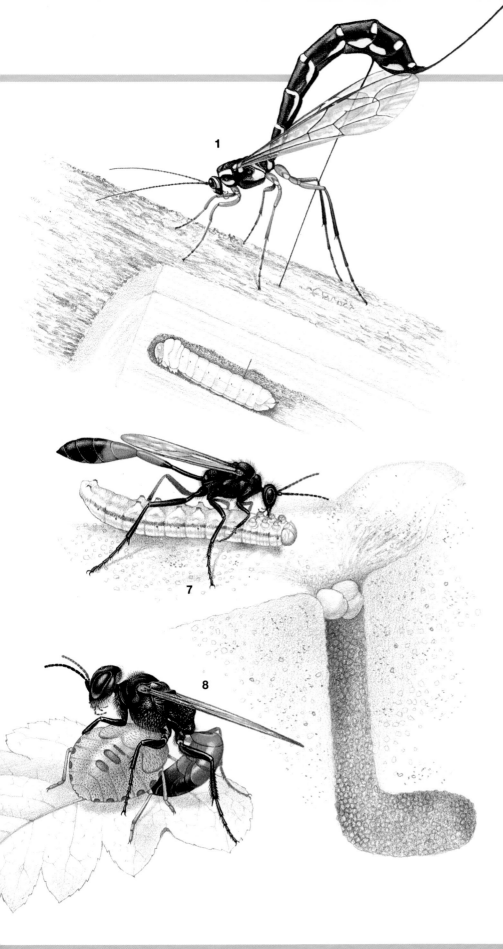

## SOCIAL WASPS

Almost all the social, or colonial, wasps are paper-making species like the yellow-jackets and hornets. These belong to the family Vespidae.

Each colony consists of one or a few egg-laying females called queens, and a larger number, often thousands, of sterile females which are known as workers. The colony is founded by one or more mated queens. These build the first few cells in the nest using a tough paper that they make from wood fibers stripped off trees and old posts. Nests may be built hanging from branches or the eaves of houses. Some species always build their nests underground.

The first generation of offspring of the queen consists of only female workers. These take over the duties of catching insect prey and extending and repairing the nest, while the queen concentrates on egg-laying. In all the vespid wasps, the eggs are laid in the cells before any food is provided. The workers supply the nest with chewed insect prey rather than whole insects. Some vespines are pests of beehives, but on balance they are beneficial as they kill a wide range of pest species for their larval food.

Eventually new queens and males are reared. These mate and the colony dies out. Only mated queens survive the winter in hibernation. They start the colony cycle again next spring.

◀Wasps at work A female ichneumon, *Rhyssa* species (1), uses her long ovipositor to lay an egg in a wood wasp larva. A weevil-hunting wasp, *Cerceris arenaria* (2), returns to her nest with prey. A spider-hunting wasp, *Sceliphron spirifex* (3), at her mud nest, watched by two parasitic wasps, a wingless female "velvet ant," *Dolichomutilla guineensis* (4), and a female jewel wasp, *Stilbum cyanurum* (5). A fly-hunter, *Mellinus arvensis* (6), with prey. An American thread-waisted wasp (*Ammophila aberti*) (7), returning with prey. A female solitary wasp, *Astata boops* (8), stings her prey, a shieldbug larva.

# ANTS

On a hot summer afternoon, the air is full of flying ants. They pour out of nests in their thousands and take to the air. These are males and females on their once-in-a-lifetime mating flights. In the air, they are not alone. Swifts and swallows swoop and glide, making the most of this flying food bonanza.

Ants are everywhere. Nevertheless, in temperate areas, most people only notice them on the few days in the year when the winged males and females stage their spectacular mating flights. In the tropics, things are different. There are thousands of species, some of them very large, and no one can fail to notice them. They get everywhere in their search for food.

## FOOD-GATHERERS, EGG-LAYERS

Ants are a special group of wasps (see pages 70-73). All ant species are social and live in colonies. Each colony has one or more egg-laying females called

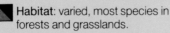

**ANTS** Order Hymenoptera: Formicidae (*about 14,000 species*)

**Habitat:** varied, most species in forests and grasslands.

**Diet:** mainly other insects, nectar, honeydew, seeds, ant-cultivated fungi.

✓ **Relationship with people:** mainly beneficial, as killers of pests.

**Distribution:** worldwide except polar regions and high mountain tops.

**Size:** length 1/25-1 1/2 in.

**Color:** mainly reddish or black.

Species mentioned in text:
Army ant (*Eciton burchelli*)
Carpenter ants (*Campanotus* species)
Common black ant (*Lasius niger*)
Common yellow ant (*Lasius flavus*)
Driver ant (*Dorylus nigricans*)
Harvester ants (*Messor* species)
Leaf-cutter ants (*Atta* species)
Long-footed ant (*Anoplolepis longipes*)
Red ants (*Myrmica* species)
Slave-maker ant (*Polyergus rufescens*)
Slow ants (*Leptothorax* species)
Weaver ants (*Oecophylla* species)
Wood ants (*Formica* species)

queens, and hundreds, thousands or even millions of workers. The workers are sterile, wingless females which, under normal circumstances, do not lay eggs. Their role is to forage for food, rear the young and defend the nest. For almost all of their lives, the queens are nothing but stay-at-home egg-laying machines.

## FOUNDING THE COLONY

After mating, a male ant soon dies. The female returns to the ground and sheds her wings. She has no need for them any more. Shortly after her flight muscles will break down to release nutrients for making eggs.

In the Common black and Common yellow ants, which live in Europe

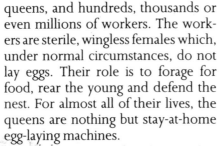

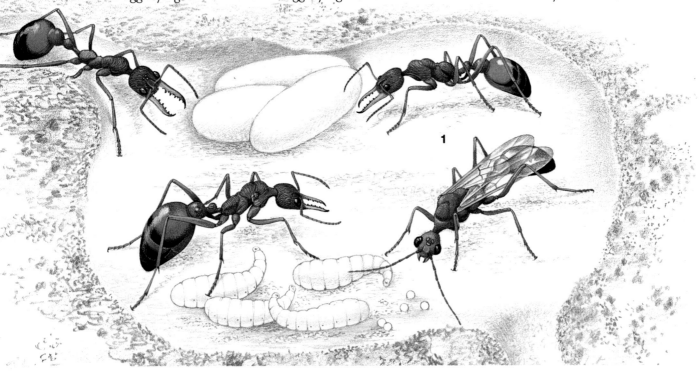

1

and North America, what happens next is typical. The queen finds a crack in the soil or a space under a log or stone and excavates a little chamber or cell. There, she lays her first batch of eggs. She does not feed, but lives off her flight muscles and body fat.

The queen guards the eggs and the larvae that hatch from them, licking them with her tongue to keep off dirt and fungal spores. She continues to lay more and more eggs, but does not collect food for the larvae. Instead, the larvae feed on the eggs constantly produced by the queen.

### JOBS IN THE HOME
After molting their skins three or four times, each larva spins a papery silk cocoon and pupates inside it. Eventually, the first generation of workers emerges. These ants extend the nest by digging out additional chambers and galleries, and they forage for food. Ants are tidy, and one of the workers' tasks is to remove droppings and other debris, and place it outside in their own garbage dump.

The workers also defend the nest against raiders from other colonies that may try to enter and steal eggs and larvae as food. Each colony has its own characteristic smell and intruders are recognized immediately.

Many ants, such as the common red species, are all armed with a sting and use this in defense. Others, like the Common black ant and the wood ants, have no sting. But they are not defenseless. They squirt out an irritating spray of formic acid from glands in their rear ends.

The Slave-maker ant raids the nests of other ant species and steals their pupae, taking them back to its own nest. It eats some of the pupae, but most hatch out and the new workers live as slaves in the colony.

### NESTS AND MOUNDS
Underground ant nests can be up to several feet deep, with tunnels and chambers on many levels. The workers tend to keep eggs and larvae in clumps of individuals of similar age. In hot weather, they move the eggs close to the soil surface to benefit from the warmth. At night and in cold weather, they take the eggs deep into the nest.

Many ant species, for example the Common yellow ant, make protective mounds of earth above their underground nests. Wood ants make their surface mounds out of pine needles. Carpenter ants are so-called because they excavate their nests in the trunks of trees. Weaver ants make their nests by weaving living leaves together. Many large workers fold over the edges of a leaf, gripping them with their jaws. At the same time smaller workers, each with a larva in its jaws, weave the leaf edges together with jets of silk squirted out by the larvae.

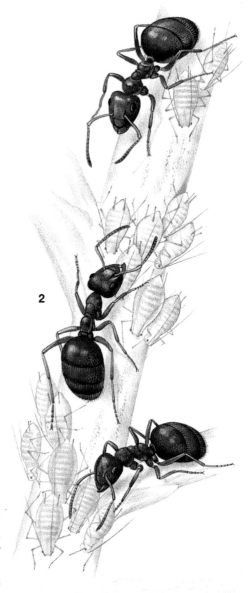

2

3

◄►**Ants at work** Wingless workers of the Australian bulldog ant (*Myrmecia gulosa*) **(1)**, tend their eggs, larvae and pupae, which are simply scattered around the nest chamber. The winged female has smaller jaws than the workers. The workers forage singly and use their powerful stings to quell insect prey. Workers of the Common black ant **(2)**, tend aphids for sweet honeydew. "Honeypot" workers of a *Myrmecocystus* species **(3)** from North America never leave the nest and act as living honey stores. Other workers feed them masses of nectar.

## ANTS ON THE MOVE

Worker ants leave the nest to forage for food. Many species are opportunists and scavenge on freshly dead insects or kill their own insect prey. If a worker has found a good source of food, it leaves a scent trail on its way back to the nest. Other workers follow this along the ground and soon appear at the feeding site.

A scent trail may attract aggressive ants and therefore some species, such as the slow ants, do not leave a trail. In these, an ant returning to a good food supply is closely followed by a second nest mate. This doubling may continue until there are as many ants on the move as in trail-laying species.

Ants on the move are a spectacular sight in tropical South America. Here, huge colonies of the Army ant are permanently traveling. Each one may have as many as 700,000 members. They march in columns, carrying their eggs and larvae with them. At night, they rest in a temporary bivouac under a rock or in a hollow tree.

## HUNTING PARTIES

An Army ant colony sends out swarm raids to hunt insects and other small animals in the leaflitter. The raiding column can be 330ft long and 25ft wide, with the leaders fanning out in front to scout for prey. It is amazing to realize that the workers are all blind; they rely entirely on scent trails laid down by the scouts. A special soldier class of workers with large jaws stands either side of the column, facing outwards, on guard.

In Africa, Driver ants have a similar way of life, but they stay longer in their resting places and often dig deep into the soil to make their nests. Their raiding columns can catch and kill prey as large as lizards and snakes.

## THE SWEET LIFE

Ants are very attracted to sweet, sugary liquids and the foragers can always be seen attending colonies of most

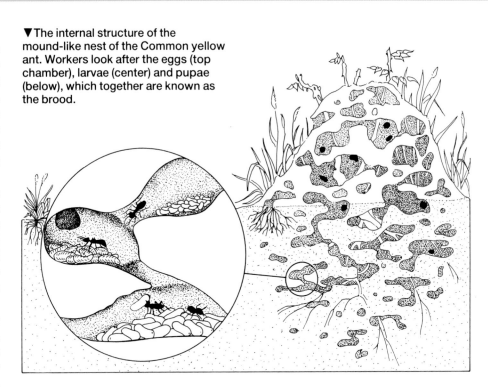

▼The internal structure of the mound-like nest of the Common yellow ant. Workers look after the eggs (top chamber), larvae (center) and pupae (below), which together are known as the brood.

▶Leaf-cutter ants return to their nest with pieces of leaf. They use these to make a compost for a fungus they eat. Like all ants, this species is capable of great feats of strength. As here, it can lift and carry pieces of leaf more than 10 times its own weight and size.

sap-sucking aphids (greenfly, black-fly), where they eat the honeydew excreted from the aphids' rear ends. They may stroke the aphids with their antennae to induce them to produce more honeydew. Ants often guard aphids from other, predatory, insects.

Back at the nest, the forager ants regurgitate liquid food for the queen and larvae. Solid food is chewed up before being passed on. Returning foragers also feed workers that look after the eggs and larvae.

The caterpillars of many of the blue butterflies produce a sweet liquid that attracts ants. Some ant species take the caterpillars into their nests. The caterpillars eat the ant larvae, but the ants seem not to mind because the caterpillars continue to provide the liquid from glands on their backs.

▲A raiding party of Army ants returns to its bivouac with a centipede it has caught. The larger workers are soldiers.

▶Workers of the Long-footed ant kill a Cocoa weevil in Papua New Guinea.

## ANTS AND PLANTS

Harvester ants forage for seeds, which they take back and store in their nests. In this way, the seeds get dispersed and some survive to grow into plants.

Violets have seeds adapted to take advantage of foraging ants, although these are species that do not normally harvest seeds. The ants cannot eat the seeds as they have hard, smooth coats. Instead, they eat little edible outgrowths from each seed. When the ants have finished eating them, they discard the seeds on their garbage dump, where they germinate.

In Central and South America, leaf-cutter ants cut out pieces of leaf which they take back to their nests. There, they chew the leaves to a pulp, which they use as a compost. On this they grow a kind of fungus that only lives in their nests and on which they feed.

# BEES

A flowery meadow hums with insect life. All the flying insects in the meadow feast at the brightly colored flowers. Hoverflies and butterflies abound. But none are as skilled as the bees in harvesting the nectar and pollen. Worker honeybees probe shallow, open flowers for nectar. The heavier bumblebees, with their longer tongues, gather nectar from the deep, tubular flowers.

▼ A female Vestal cuckoo bumblebee feeds on wild thyme. Cuckoo bees lay eggs in the nests of other bees. They have no workers and no pollen baskets.

**BEES** Superfamily Apoidea
*(at least 20,000 species)*

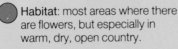

Habitat: most areas where there are flowers, but especially in warm, dry, open country.

Diet: pollen and nectar, plant oils, glandular secretions of workers (honeybee larvae).

✓ Relationship with people: beneficial as major pollinators of important crops and natural vegetation.

Distribution: worldwide; most numerous in warm, dry areas, such as semi-deserts.

Size: length ⅔-1⅔in.

Color: from black to brilliant metallic blue and green; many species with conspicuous bands of white, yellow and black hairs.

Species mentioned in text:
Bumblebees (*Bombus* species)
Dogtooth violet bee (*Andrena erythronii*)
Heather mining bee (*Colletes succinctus*)
Honeybees (*Apis* species)
Mason bees (*Osmia* species)
Red snail bee (*Hoplitis lhotellieri*)
Tawny mining bee (*Andrena fulva*)
Vestal cuckoo bumblebee (*Psithyrus vestalis*)
Western or Domestic honeybee (*Apis mellifera*)

◄A swarm of Western, or Domestic, honeybees clusters on a pine while scout workers seek out a new nest site.

Bumblebees and honeybees are social insects. They live in colonial nests. Each colony is a family unit, with a single, egg-laying female, the queen, and a few hundred to many thousands of workers. As in the ants and social wasps, the workers are a special caste of sterile females. They rear young, guard and maintain the nest and forage for food. The vast majority of

▼ The three castes of a honeybee colony. A male or drone (a), with large eyes meeting on top of the head. A sterile female or worker (b), and the queen (c), with her enlarged abdomen filled with eggs.

the world's bee species, however, are solitary creatures and do not live in colonies. Their nests are made by a single female working alone.

## A TWO-WAY RELATIONSHIP

Bees are really a special group of hunting wasps that have become vegetarians. Instead of providing their young with insect prey, they collect pollen from flowers.

Bees probably arose in the middle of the Cretaceous period (135 to 65 million years ago), when flowering plants first appeared. The evolution of flowering plants and bees went hand in hand. Flowers came to depend on

insects for fertilization by the accidental transfer of pollen from one flower to another. It pays flowers to attract insect visitors by providing rewards for their unwitting services: an excess of pollen as food, and also sugary nectar. Scents and colorful, showy petals make them attractive to insects.

At the same time, bees became the most efficient insects at exploiting what flowers have to offer. They have long tongues for sucking up nectar, and their bodies are covered with branched hairs, among which pollen grains become trapped. They remove the pollen by grooming actions and transfer it to a special structure for carrying it back to the nest.

## SOLITARY MINERS AND MASONS

Many solitary bees dig nest burrows in the ground. They are called mining bees, and often thousands of them nest in dense aggregations. One of the commonest in Europe is the Tawny mining bee, which appears in spring and often nests in lawns. The Dog-tooth violet bee, is a common North American species.

In its burrow, at the end of a side branch, the female mining bee hollows out a smooth-walled chamber, or cell, which she lines with a waterproof secretion from a gland in her abdomen. In the cell she stores a mixture of pollen and nectar shaped into a tiny ball. She transports the pollen back to the nest on a "scopa," which is a brush of special hairs on each hind leg. She then lays a single egg on the pollen ball before sealing the cell with a plug of soil. There is enough food for the whole of larval growth. As with all solitary bees, the female never lives to see her offspring.

Female mason bees by contrast, use as nests existing cavities such as beetle borings in wood, or hollow

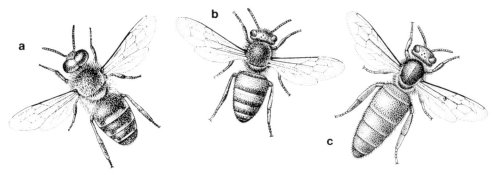

▲A female Heather mining bee leaves her nest in an earth bank. The three cells, seen in section, contain a runny mixture of heather pollen and nectar. Two of the cells contain an egg attached to the wall.

◄Some female mason bees nest only in empty snail shells. This Red snail bee puts the finishing touch to its nest by sealing it with pieces of broken shell.

plant stems. They do not line their cells with a secretion, but instead use, according to species, small pebbles, mud, resin, chewed leaf material or plant or even animal hairs.

## AN EGG-LAYING MACHINE

In cool countries, the plump, furry bumblebees are the most familiar social bees. They nest either underground, often in old mouse nests, or above ground, in dense tussocks of tall grass.

A bumblebee colony has an annual cycle, starting off with a single fertilized female, or queen. She emerges in spring after a winter spent in hibernation. At first, she lives like a solitary bee, collecting pollen and nectar for herself and her offspring. She stores pollen and rears her offspring in little cells of wax secreted by glands in her abdomen.

The first of the adult bumblebees to emerge are workers, which are smaller than the queen but are otherwise very similar to her. Like her, they have a pollen basket on the outer face of their hind legs. Once they have emerged, the queen no longer ventures from the nest. She remains inside as an egg-laying machine.

In summer, the queen lays unfertilized eggs that develop into males. At the same time, some larvae receive extra food and develop into queens. They mate with the males and then seek out a suitable place in which to hibernate. The males and the rest of the colony die out with the first frosts of the fall. Only the newly mated queens survive the winter to start a new nesting cycle the next spring.

## FED ON ROYAL JELLY

Honeybee colonies are perennial, and a queen can live for up to 5 years. A honeybee nest consists of several double-sided vertical combs of six-sided cells. The honeybees store pollen and honey in the cells and also rear their young in them.

Wild colonies build nests in hollow trees or in rock clefts. Beekeepers provide their bees with artificial nests called hives.

The organization of a honeybee colony is fascinating and complicated. There is a single queen and up to 80,000 workers. The queen lays up to 1,500 eggs a day and has a kind of chemical control over her workers. She secretes a scent, or pheromone, called queen substance from glands in her head. This prevents the workers from producing eggs themselves. It also stops them from rearing new queens and encourages them to forage for food. Because the queen is always attended by a large "court" of

▲ ▶ **Honeybee hive and dances** Worker honeybees tend larvae in a section of comb (above), while a returned forager tells her nestmates that she has found a food source within 80ft of the nest by performing a "round dance" (1). Another worker performs the "waggle dance" (2). During the straight run, she waggles her abdomen, which indicates not only the distance of a food source more than 80ft away, but also its direction. The angle of the straight run from the vertical is the same as the angle between the Sun and the food source, as seen from the hive entrance.

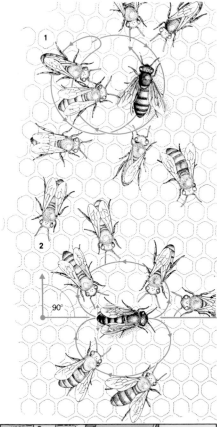

workers that constantly lick her and touch her with their antennae, the queen substance very quickly spreads among all the workers.

The tasks performed by a worker are related to her age. She spends her first 3 days as a cleaner. Then she is a nurse and feeds larvae on "royal jelly" produced by glands in her head. All larvae receive this for their first 3 days, after which they are fed honey and pollen. Only larvae destined to be queens continue to be fed only on royal jelly. Next, at about 10 days, the worker becomes a builder, for now wax glands in her abdomen grow in size. After this, she and others of similar age guard the nest entrance for a few days. For the rest of her life of 6 weeks, she is a field bee, gathering nectar and pollen from flowers.

# SCORPIONS

As the sands of the Arizona desert cool down at dusk, a night shift of small creatures emerges. From under stones and out of burrows they come – mice, centipedes and beetles. And among them a female scorpion scuttles in search of insect prey. Soon, she finds a grasshopper. In an instant, the scorpion grasps the insect in her claws. She quells its struggles with a killing stab from the sting in her tail.

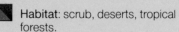

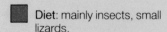
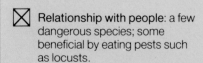

## SCORPIONS Subclass
Scorpiones (*about 1,200 species*)

**Habitat:** scrub, deserts, tropical forests.

**Diet:** mainly insects, small lizards.

**Relationship with people:** a few dangerous species; some beneficial by eating pests such as locusts.

**Distribution:** worldwide, in warm temperate and tropical regions.

**Size:** True scorpions: length 1/3-7in. Whip scorpions: length 1/3-2in. Sun spiders: length 1/3-2in. Harvestmen: length 1/25-2/3in.

**Color:** pale straw, through fawn to dark brown and black.

**Species mentioned in text:**
Arizona scorpion (*Hadrurus arizonensis*)
Austral scorpion (*Androctonus australis*)
Desert scorpions (*Paruroctonus* species)
Durango scorpion (*Centruoides suffusus*)
Giant American whip scorpion (*Mastigoproctus giganteus*)

The reputation of true scorpions as killers is only partly deserved. For although they all have a venomous sting, very few pose a threat to humans. At worst, a typical sting is no more painful or dangerous than that of a wasp or hornet. Nevertheless, the habit of inspecting one's shoes each morning when in scorpion country may prevent a painful surprise.

There are some species, though, which can inflict a fatal sting. The Durango scorpion from Mexico can kill a person, and the Austral scorpion of North Africa has a venom as powerful as that of a cobra. Its sting will kill a dog as large as an Alsatian in 7 minutes and an adult human after 6 or 7 hours.

### KILLING MACHINES
Scorpions have had at least 3 million years in which to perfect this killing power. The oldest of all arthropod fossils is a scorpion and they were possibly the very first arthropods to conquer the land.

Scorpions, like their arachnid relatives the spiders, have eight legs. They appear in fact to have 10 legs, but the front pair of "legs," which bear a pair of grasping pincers, are really massively enlarged pedipalps.

The body of a scorpion has two main sections, the prosoma and the abdomen. There is no distinct head

▲Lurking on a branch, this scorpion awaits unsuspecting prey with pincers poised. The sting is at the tip of the tail.

region, and the prosoma, which bears the mouth, is covered with a horny carapace. Just in front of the mouth is a pair of three-segmented biting jaws called chelicerae.

Scorpions have a pair of simple eyes in the middle of the carapace, and between 2 and 5 pairs of small eyes near its front edge. The sex organs and genital opening are on the underside of the first abdominal segment.

Directly behind the single genital opening are tiny structures unique to scorpions, the pectines. These are a pair of comb-like structures that touch the ground as the scorpion walks. They detect vibrations caused by prey, and are very sensitive. Desert scorpions can detect a burrowing cockroach from a distance of 20in. It is possible that the pectines also allow the scorpion to assess the texture of the ground.

The scorpion uses its pincers to grab and hold on to prey while it arches its tail forward to inject venom. The venom is a nerve poison and it has an instant effect on insects, which are the main prey of scorpions.

Scorpions have a very thick, tough cuticle. This protects the soft tissues and is almost completely waterproof. In desert-dwelling scorpions, it prevents the loss of too much body fluid. In extreme heat, species such as the Arizona scorpion burrow in the sand as far down as 35in to keep cool.

Not all scorpions are desert animals. Many species like damp conditions and live in rain forests. Close relatives of scorpions, the harvestmen, are common in temperate regions.

▲A relative of true scorpions, this sun or wind spider crushes to death insects and small lizards with its huge chelicerae. It lacks poison glands.

▼This large harvestman stalks prey on a leaf in Venezuela. It uses its large fang-like chelicerae to seize insects. Harvestmen have just two eyes, not the four pairs of most sighted arachnids.

## MATING AND MATERNAL CARE

Before mating, scorpions have a long courtship. The pair face each other with tails uplifted and circle around. The male then seizes the female with his pincers and they walk backwards and forwards together for hours.

Eventually, the male deposits a sperm package, or spermatophore, on the ground. He then maneuvers his mate so that her genital opening is just over the spermatophore and she can take the sperm into her body.

Female scorpions lay between 1 and 95 eggs. The eggs soon hatch and the young scorpions climb onto their mother's back, where they stay until after their first molt.

## WHIP SCORPIONS

The relatives of scorpions include sun or wind spiders (subclass Solifugae), harvestmen (Opiliones) and the whip scorpions. The latter are mainly tropical and have no sting in their whip-like tails. Whip scorpions like the Giant American species are often called vinegaroons because when disturbed, they spray their enemies with acetic acid. They walk on only three pairs of legs. The front pair are long and thin and used as "feelers."

# SPIDERS

A young spider stands on tiptoe at the top of a grass stem. With its abdomen tilted upwards, it releases a fine silk thread into the breeze. The silk rises in the warm air and soon exerts a strong pull on the animal. The spiderling lets go and drifts up into the air, carried aloft by its thread.

The spider's action is usually known as ballooning and it is a good way of traveling far without using much energy. Ballooning is the reason why spiders are among the earliest colonizers of new islands that have arisen out of the sea because of volcanic action. Indeed, spiders are the most successful of the non-insect arthropods. They have invaded almost all parts of the world and live in almost all habitats.

Spiders all catch and eat living prey comprising mainly insects. However, birds, frogs, and even fish, form part of the diet of some species.

## BUILT FOR SUCCESS

The body of a spider has two main parts: the cephalothorax and the abdomen. The cephalothorax consists of a combined head and thorax region covered with a hardened shield called a carapace. It bears four pairs of legs. The mouth is at the front of the underside and is flanked by a pair of fangs called chelicerae. These are used in feeding, defense and, sometimes, for digging. A poison gland opens into the the tip of each chelicera. When feeding, the spider uses its fangs to inject a killing poison into prey. It then injects digestive juices, which reduce the prey's tissues to a liquid on which the spider feeds.

▶A lynx spider eats a termite in Kenya. Most of these spiders are green and sit motionless on leaves until an unwary insect wanders by. Lynx spiders are skilled at leaping from leaf to leaf.

**SPIDERS** Subclass Araneae
*(at least 30,000 species)*

▰ **Habitat:** almost everywhere, from deserts to houses.

▰ **Diet:** mainly insects; a few species eat fish, small lizards, birds.

☑ **Relationship with people:** a few dangerous species, but most are beneficial because they kill insect pests.

**Distribution:** worldwide, except Antarctica.

**Size:** body length 1/35-3½in, legspan up to 10½in.

**Color:** varied, from black, mottled grays and browns, to red, green.

Species mentioned in text:
Baboon spiders (*Harpactira* species)
Black widow spider (*Latrodectus mactans*)
Bolas spiders (*Mastophora* species)
Brown recluse spider (*Loxosceles reclusa*)
Common garden spider (*Araneus diadematus*)
Dark garden wolf spider (*Pardosa pullata*)
Large house spider (*Tegenaria gigantea*)
Lynx spiders (*Peucetia* species)
Orb spiders (*Argiope* species)
Raft spider (*Dolomedes fimbriatus*)
Spitting spider (*Scytodes thoracica*)
Sydney funnel-web spider (*Atrax robustus*)

The chelicerae are flanked by a pair of pedipalps, which are appendages sensitive to touch and taste. Spiders use these in the same way as insects use their antennae. Male spiders use their pedipalps as a sperm store and for introducing sperm into the body of the female during mating.

Spiders have usually eight simple eyes on the front of their cephalothorax. The jumping spiders and the net-casting spiders all have excellent sight, better than in any other land invertebrates. The abdomen contains the heart, gut, respiratory system, sex organs and the silk glands.

## SILK

Silk is very important in the lives of all spiders, even in those species that do not spin the familiar thread webs.

Silk is a special kind of protein. Spiders make it in glands near the tip of the abdomen. They use their legs to draw out the silk from the spinnerets, which are hollow finger-like projections at the tip of the abdomen. The liquid silk hardens as it is drawn out. The threads are stronger than steel threads of the same diameter, and can be stretched for up to one-third of their length without breaking. This is amazing considering that the finest silk threads are less than $\frac{1}{50,000}$in across and the thickest are only four times greater than this!

Most spiders start life surrounded by silk. The female encloses her batch of eggs in a protective sac of silk. Many species hide their egg sacs in crevices and never see their offspring. Some, though, like the Dark garden wolf

▲A baboon spider from South Africa. Although one of the so-called bird-eating spiders, large insects and small lizards are the more usual prey of this species.

▼An orb spider straddles its web. The web is conspicuous to birds so that they avoid blundering into, and damaging, it.

spider, carry their egg sacs around with them, attached to the spinnerets. Each female will defend her egg sac to the death. When the 40 or so eggs hatch, the spiderlings climb on her back and remain there until their first molt. After this they leave their mother and fend for themselves.

## CAUGHT IN A WEB

Spiders usually show their presence by their webs, which they use to trap insect prey. The cobwebs found in houses are usually the sheet webs of the Large house spider. This is the hairy, mottled gray species that so often ends up in the bath.

The Garden spider is responsible for the beautiful orb (disc-like) webs that fill the spaces between plants in late summer and the fall. Webs of this type are covered with sticky droplets that help to trap any insects that blunder into them. The vibrations caused by the struggling insect alert the spider, which runs across the web and kills the prey.

## OTHER FEEDING METHODS

The bolas spiders of North America catch insects in a very unusual way. Each spider hangs horizontally from a silk thread slung underneath a twig. It draws out a 2in-length of silk and

attaches a bead-sized droplet of sticky gum at the end. Somehow, the spider can sense the presence of, say, an approaching moth and swings the silk line in its direction. The spider's aim is such that the sticky droplet of gum hits the moth, which is then pulled to within reach of the deadly fangs.

The Spitting spider of Europe and North America catches insect prey by spitting out two thin streams of sticky gum through its chelicerae. These streams move from side to side, so the insect is stuck down firmly by two zigzag lines of sticky thread.

Apart from the egg sac, wolf spiders have little use for silk. They do not

spin a web in which to trap prey. Instead, they roam over the ground and actively hunt small insects.

## DANGEROUS SPECIES

Many people have an instinctive fear of spiders, but this is hardly justified. Only a very few of the 30,000 species pose any threat. The Black widow is one of them and is found in most warm countries. Its bite causes great pain and paralysis of the muscles. If the muscles involved in breathing are affected, the bitten person may die.

The poison of the Brown recluse of North America kills tissues around the bite. The effect can spread to become a gaping black wound 6in across, which takes a long time to heal.

A bite from the notorious Sydney funnel-web spider of south-eastern Australia can also be fatal. It results in a massive build-up of fluid in the lungs, leading eventually to coma and death. As with the Black widow's bite, an antipoison is available.

◄By dangling its front feet as bait into the water from a leaf raft, this Raft spider has caught a minnow.

▶**Typical spider behavior** A female Raft spider **(1)** carries her egg sac. A male jumping spider, *Evarcha arcuata* **(2)**, courts a female, right, with movements of his front legs. A male orb spider, *Araneus quadratus* **(3)**, right, vibrates the female's web in such a way that she recognizes him as a mate not prey. An orb spider, *Argiope bruennichi* **(4)**, with warning coloration, sits in the middle of her web.

# TICKS, MITES

After 7 years without a meal, a female Sheep tick crawls up a tall grass stem. Her wait is nearly over, for a sheep brushes past. The tick climbs aboard, crawls through the fleece to the skin, and sinks her piercing mouthparts into the sheep. Now she makes up for lost time and sucks blood continuously for 9 days. Eventually, she drops to the ground and lays several thousand eggs.

Ticks are members of the class Arachnida and are related to spiders; they have eight legs and there is no division between the front part of the body, the prosoma, and the hind part, or abdomen.

Ticks use their toothed chelicerae to puncture the host's skin. They suck up blood with a snout-like projection, the hypostome, after injecting saliva that contains several anticoagulants to prevent the blood from clotting.

### FASTING AND FEASTING
The ability to withstand long periods without food is part of the secret of the success of ticks. The chance is very slight that a warm-blooded mammal will just happen to brush against the stem on which a hungry tick waits. Patient fasting is not only a virtue of the adults, for the six-legged larvae, or seed-ticks, which hatch from the eggs, can survive without a blood meal for 6 to 15 months.

If the tick larvae are to molt and become eight-legged nymphs, a meal is necessary. Should the larvae survive and develop into nymphs, they can do without food for a whole year. To become adults, the nymphs must have one final meal before they molt.

The growth and development of ticks is thus a long drawn-out affair, alternating between long periods of

## TICKS, MITES
Subclass Acari (*30,000 species*)

    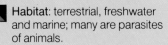

**Habitat:** terrestrial, freshwater and marine; many are parasites of animals.

**Diet:** many feed on living plants, others scavenge; ticks feed entirely on blood of reptiles, birds or mammals.

**Relationship with people:** many irritating species and some harmful by spreading disease; many beneficial in soil.

**Distribution:** worldwide.

**Size:** length 1/30-1 1/4in.

**Color:** mainly brown or black, but red, green and yellow common.

**Species mentioned in text:**
Beetle mites (Order Cryptostigmata)
Fowl tick (*Argas persicus*)
House dust mite (*Dermatophagoides pteronissinus*)
Human follicle mite (*Demodex folliculorum*)
Itch or Scabies mite (*Sarcoptes scabei*)
Sheep tick (*Ixodes ricinus*)

◄Sheep ticks suck the blood of a hibernating hedgehog. These hard ticks have mouthparts for hanging on to the moving host while feeding.

►A giant "red velvet" mite in Kenya. This is a free-living species. Most mites are parasites of plants or animals.

starvation and short periods of plenty, when feeding is frenzied and almost continuous.

With such a chancy life-style, it is not surprising that 99.8 percent of ticks never survive to become adults. However, each female lays thousands of eggs and it has been calculated that in parts of North America there may be as many as 2½ million ticks to the sq mi. With such huge numbers, enough ticks will be able to feed and therefore breed each year.

## HARD- OR SOFT-BODIED

The Sheep tick is the species most likely to bother people, especially in Europe. As well as living on sheep and humans, it also feeds on many kinds of birds and small mammals, including hedgehogs. When fully fed, the body of the female Sheep tick expands to about ⅓in long and looks like a smooth, blue pea.

The Sheep tick belongs to a group known as the "hard ticks," which get their name from the horny protective shield, or scutum, on top of the front of the body. "Soft ticks" do not have this plate. They live in the nests of their hosts, and include such species as the Fowl tick. This is a pest of hens in warm, dry parts of the world.

## TICKS AND DISEASE

Ticks can be dangerous to people because they spread diseases by transporting viruses and bacteria from infected hosts. The worst diseases are kinds of encephalitis, in which the patient has high fever, and inflammation of the brain that often results in paralysis.

Animals with high infestations of ticks can become very weak and even die because of severe blood loss. This fact was used as a means of execution by people of the Turkman and Uzbek tribes in Asia. A prisoner would be chained to a wall and then thousands of starved soft ticks were introduced into the cell. Death was particularly slow and agonizing.

## EVER-PRESENT MITES

Related to the ticks, and often looking like minute versions of them, are the mites. There are about 29,000 species and they live in all parts of the world, including polar regions and the highest of mountains. Some are free-living and prey on small worms and insect eggs. The so-called beetle mites live in soil and leaf litter. They are the most numerous mites and are very useful

because they feed on decaying plant material and so return nutrients to the soil.

Many species live in close association with nesting animals and feed on nest debris. The House dust mite lives in houses and eats house dust, which is almost entirely made up of flakes of skin, which we shed all the time. Some people are allergic to this mite, a reaction that causes asthma.

Some species, like the tiny Itch, or Scabies, mite, burrow into the skin of people, causing terrible itching and a red rash. Others, like the Human follicle mite, live in our hair follicles, where they eat the oily secretion sebum. They are less than ¹⁄₅₀in long and, although all of us have them, especially in the follicles of our eyelashes, they are too small for us to feel their movements.

# GLOSSARY

**Abdomen** The hind part of the body of an arthropod, behind the thorax and containing the gut and sex organs.

**Adaptation** Features of an animal's body or life-style that suit it to its environment.

**Antennae** The "feelers" of an arthropod, which are sensitive to touch and contain the sense of smell.

**Appendage** Any limb or jointed outgrowth of the body, such as antennae, legs or wings.

**Aquatic** Living in water.

**Arachnid** A member of the class Arachnida, which contains the spiders, scorpions, ticks and mites.

**Arthropod** An invertebrate with jointed limbs and a hard exoskeleton, a body plan which probably evolved independently on several occasions.

**Book lung** A chamber inside the abdomen of arachnids where the exchange of gases in breathing takes place across folded leaf-like plates which have a rich blood supply.

**Brood cell** A specially made chamber in the nest of a wasp or bee in which food is stored, an egg is laid and the larva completes its development.

**Camouflage** A color pattern that closely resembles the background on which an animal usually rests; this makes it difficult for predators to see.

**Caste** In colonies of social insects, any group of individuals that are built differently and behave differently from other groups in the same nest, such as the "soldier" caste of ants and termites and the workers of ants and honeybees.

**Cephalothorax** The fused head and thorax of an arachnid (= prosoma).

**Chitin** The tough, waterproof, horny substance which forms the cuticle or exoskeleton of arthropods.

**Chrysalis** The pupa stage of moths and butterflies, which is often protected by a tough cocoon of silk.

**Claspers** A pair of pincer-like appendages at the tip of the abdomen of male insects, which are used to grip the female during mating.

**Cocoon** The protective silk envelope spun by the last larval stage of many insects just before pupation.

**Colony** A group of social insects that shares the same nest.

**Comb** The ranks of brood and food-storage cells in the nests of social wasps and bees.

**Complete metamorphosis** Where development goes through three stages – egg, larva and pupa – before the adult stage is reached.

**Compound eye** An eye made of hundreds or even thousands of units (facets), each of which has its own lens and nerve connection to the brain and which gives a mosaic kind of image.

**Courtship** Special behavior that may involve characteristic "dance" movements, the production of scents or sounds, or even the presentation of "love gifts," which enables a male and female of a species to recognize one another and assess each other's suitability as a mate.

**Crustacean** A member of the phylum Crustacea, which includes crabs, lobsters, shrimps, barnacles and woodlice.

**Cuticle** The hard, external shell enclosing the body of arthropods, made of chitin.

**Drone** A male honeybee (*Apis* species).

**Endopterygote** An insect in which the wings develop internally and in which there is a pupal stage, that is complete metamorphosis.

**Epidermis** The single layer of living cells which underlies and secretes the cuticle of an arthropod.

**Exopterygote** An insect in which the wings develop externally and in which there is no pupal stage but a series of nymphs, that is incomplete metamorphosis.

**Exoskeleton** The external skeleton or shell of an arthropod, made of a chitinous cuticle.

**Flash coloration** Brightly colored parts of an animal's body which are normally hidden, but which can be displayed suddenly to startle and frighten away a predator.

**Fungus comb** A mass of fungus grown by fungus termites and leaf-cutter ants, on which the insects always feed.

**Gall** A special growth of plant tissue which can be stimulated by the presence of a virus, fungus, mite or insect egg. Galls caused by insects grow in size and the larva feeds on special tissues inside.

**Genitalia** The hard parts of an arthropod's reproductive system, which are engaged during mating.

**Gill** In insects, the thin-skinned outgrowths of the bodies of aquatic larvae, across which the gas exchanges of respiration take place.

**Gland** A special tissue or group of tissues which makes a substance such as a scent.

**Halteres** The modified, club-shaped hindwings of true flies (Diptera), which have a sensory role while the insect is in flight.

**Herbivore** An animal that eats mainly plants.

**Incomplete metamorphosis** The kind of development in some groups of insects where there is no pupal stage. The egg hatches to produce a larva or nymph which molts several times before becoming adult. The larva resembles a miniature adult and the wings develop externally.

**Insectivore** An animal or plant that feeds on insects.

**Instar** The stage between two molts in immature arthropods.

**Mimicry** Where members of one species (the mimic) are protected from predators by resembling the appearance of another species (the model).

**Myriapod** A member of the superclass Myriapoda, which includes the millipedes and centipedes.

**Nectar** A sweet, sugary liquid secreted by plants to attract pollinating insects.

**Nymph** An old word for the larvae of insects which have an incomplete metamorphosis.

**Ovipositor** The egg-laying tube in female insects.

**Pedipalp** An appendage in Chelicerates used either to seize prey (scorpions), to introduce sperm into the female (male spiders), or as sensory structures (female spiders).

**Pheromone** A chemical messenger or scent given off by one individual of a species and which affects the behavior of other members of the same species, e.g., the alarm pheromone of honeybees, the sex pheromones of courting moths.

**Phylum** In animal classification, the major grouping below Kingdom and Sub-kingdom.

**Pollen grains** The male sex cells of flowering plants, produced in structures called anthers.

**Pollination** The accidental transport of pollen by insects from the male parts (anthers) of one flower to the female parts (stigmas) of another flower of the same species. Some plants are adapted to be pollinated by wind, birds or bats.

**Predator** An animal that preys on other animals for food.

**Prolegs** "False" unjointed legs of some insect larvae.

**Prothorax** The first of the three segments making up the thorax of an insect.

**Pupa, pupal stage** The non-feeding and usually inactive stage between the larva and adult in insects with a complete metamorphosis. During this stage most larval tissues break down and reform into adult tissues.

**Royal jelly, Bee milk** A special, rich food made by glands in the heads of honeybee workers and fed to the larvae. All larvae receive this for their first three days, those destined to become queens receive this food exclusively for the whole of their development.

**Scale** A modified hair of an insects, which is broad and flat.

**Segment** A unit of an arthropod's body or appendage which is similar to other, adjacent units.

**Social** Living together in a colony.

**Soldier** A special kind of worker, usually larger than other workers and with big jaws, found in the colonies of some termites and ants. It defends other workers and the nest.

**Species** A group of animals of the same structure which can breed with one another.

**Spiracle** The external opening of a breathing tube or trachea in an arthropod.

**Terrestrial** Living on land.

**Thorax** The body region of an arthropod that is between the head and abdomen. In insects it bears the wings, legs and their muscles.

**Trachea** A breathing tube found in millipedes, centipedes, some spiders and all insects, which is lined with cuticle and leads by many fine branches to all parts of the body from a breathing hole or spiracle.

**Warning coloration** Bright, conspicuous color patterns in poisonous or foul-tasting insects. Insectivorous reptiles, birds and mammals learn to associate this with an unpleasant experience and avoid insects patterned in this way.

**Worker** A sterile, non-reproductive member of an insect colony, responsible for care of the brood, nest building and repair, defense and foraging. Worker termites can be male or female, but in ants, wasps and bees, workers are always females.

# INDEX

## Scientific names

The first name of each double-barrel Latin name refers to the *Genus*, the second to the *species*. Single names not in *italic* refer to a class, subclass, order, family or sub-family and are cross referenced to the Common name index.

94

# FURTHER READING

Alexander, R. McNeill (1979), *The Invertebrates*, Cambridge University Press, Cambridge, England.

Alexander, R. McNeill (ed) (1986), *The Encyclopedia of Animal Biology*, Facts On File, New York.

Arnett, R.H. (1985), *American Insects: A Handbook of the Insects of America North of Mexico*, Van Nostrand Reinhold, New York.

Barnes, R.D. (1982), *Invertebrate Zoology*, 4th edn, Holt-Saunders, Philadelphia.

Barrington, E.J.W. (1982), *Invertebrate Structure and Function*, Van Nostrand Reinhold, New York.

Berry, R.J. and Hallam, A. (eds) (1986), *The Encyclopedia of Animal Evolution*, Facts On File, New York.

Brian, M.V. (1983), *Social Insects, Ecology and Behavioural Biology*, Chapman and Hall, London and New York.

Daly, H.V., Dayen, J.T. and Erlich, P.R. (1978), *Introduction to Insect Biology and Diversity*, McGraw-Hill, New York.

Eisner, T. and Wilson, E.O. (eds) (1977), *The Insects: Readings from Scientific American*, W.H.Freeman, San Francisco.

Foelix, R.F. (1982), *Biology of Spiders*, Harvard University Press, Cambridge, Massachusetts.

Frisch, K. von (1967), *The Dance Language and Orientation of Bees*, (trans. L.E. Chadwick) Belknap Press of Harvard University Press, Cambridge, Massachusetts.

Gillott, C. (1980), *Entomology*, Plenum, New York and London.

Linsenmaier, W. (1972), *Insects of the World* (trans. L.E. Chadwick), McGraw-Hill, New York and London.

Moore, P.D. (ed) (1986), *The Encyclopedia of Animal Ecology*, Facts On File, New York.

O'Toole, C. (ed) (1986), *The Encyclopedia of Insects*, Facts On File, New York.

Slater, P.J.B. (ed) (1986), *The Encyclopedia of Animal Behavior*, Facts On File, New York.

# ACKNOWLEDGMENTS

### Picture credits

Key: *t* top. *b* bottom. *c* center. *l* left. *r* right.
Abbreviations: A Ardea. ANT Australasian Nature Transparencies. BCL Bruce Coleman Ltd. CAH C.A. Henley. NHPA Natural History Photographic Agency. NSP Natural Science Photos. OSF Oxford Scientific Films. P Premaphotos. PEP Planet Earth Pictures. SPL Science Photo Library.

8, 9 NHPA/A. Bannister. 10 CAH. 11*tl* NHPA/S. Dalton. 11*tr*, P. 11*c* BCL. 12-13, 13 P. 14 CAH. 15 NHPA/S. Dalton. 16-17, 20, 21, 22 P. 23*t* Mark Collins. 23*b* 24, 25*t,b*, 26-27 P. 27 OSF/J. Cooke. 28, 30-31 P. 32 NHPA/S. Dalton. 33*t* ANT. 33*b* CAH. 34 OSF/M. Fogden. 35 P. 38 R. Robinson. 39*t* OSF/D. Shale. 39*b* Biophoto Associates. 42 P. 43 ANT/K. Atkinson. 44, 45, 48, 49*t,b*, 50, 51 P. 52 OSF/G. Bernard. 53 OSF/Peter Parks. 56*t* CAH. 56*b* OSF/T. Shepherd. 57 P. 58-59 OSF/G. Bernard. 59 P. 60 NHPA/A. Bannister. 61*t,b* P. 63 NHPA/S. Dalton. 65, 66-67, 68 P. 69*t* M. Fogden. 69*b* P. 70 Agence Nature. 71, 76, 77*t* P. 77*b* PEP/C. Prior. 78, 79, 80 P. 81 A. 82 PEP/J.M. King. 82-83 OSF/S. Dalton. 83, 84, 85*t* P. 85*b* M. Fogden. 86 SPL/Martin Dohrn. 88 NSP/J.A. Grant. 89 P.

### Artwork credits.

Key: *t* top. *b* bottom. *c* center. *l* left. *r* right.
Abbreviations: DO Denys Ovenden. RL Richard Lewington. SD Simon Driver

6/7 SD. 7, 8 RL. 10, 15 SD. 18, 19 RL. 20 DO. 22*t* SD. 22*b*, 26, 29, 30 RL. 36-37 DO. 39 Keith Shannon. 40-41 RL. 43 Oxford Illustrators Ltd. 45, 46-47 RL. 53 SD. 54, 55, 62-63, 64-65, 72-73, 74-75 RL. 76 Keith Shannon. 79, 80, 81, 87 RL.